CREATING SPACES AND
FINDING VOICES

SUNY Series on Teacher Preparation and Development
Alan R. Tom, Editor

CREATING SPACES AND FINDING VOICES

Teachers Collaborating for Empowerment

Janet L. Miller

STATE UNIVERSITY OF NEW YORK PRESS

Published by
State University of New York Press, Albany

For information, address State University of New York
Press, State University Plaza, Albany, N.Y., 12246

Library of Congress Cataloging-in-Publication Data

Miller, Janet L., 1945—
    Creating spaces and finding voices : teachers collaborating for
empowerment / Janet L. Miller
        p.   cm. — (SUNY series on teacher preparation and
development)
    Includes bibliographical references.
    ISBN 0-7914-0281-9. — ISBN 0-7914-0282-7 (pbk.)
    1. Teaching—United States.   2. Teachers—United States—
Attitudes.   I. Title.   II. Series.
LB1775.M615   1990
371.1′02′0973—dc20   89-36216
                                                   CIP

10 9 8 7 6 5

To the five teacher-researchers
and their courage to challenge and create

CONTENTS

CONTENTS

Introduction

This book chronicles the shared journey of five classroom teachers and myself, a university professor, as we examine the possibilities and dilemmas of collaborative inquiry and teacher empowerment. The narrative focuses on explorations of our daily practice. Within those explorations, we attempt collaborative reflections on the contexts and assumptions that influence and frame our practice.

The narrative also details our attempts to conduct forms of inquiry within our classrooms and within our group that extend the concept of teacher-as-researcher into reciprocal and interactive forms. In chronicling nearly three years of our meetings, our written exchanges, and our evolving questions, this narrative of collaboration also portrays our efforts to challenge not only technical-rational modes of research but also deficit models of teacher development. We constantly grapple with conceptions of empowerment that only emphasize improvement of teachers' decision-making skills or that assume equitable and willing participation in dialogue.

When we gathered together in the summer of 1986, none of us had any idea of the forms that our exploratory, teacher-researcher collaboration might take. We certainly did not anticipate that our evolution as a group might appear in book form. As we began to share our stories with others, in classrooms and in the corridors of our schools, and eventually at several meetings and conferences, other educators began to question us about the specifics of our collaborative intentions and procedures. We could only respond with descriptions of the tentative and fluctuating processes of our questions, discussions, and writings. As we described these processes and their emerging effects on our daily lives as teachers, others began to press for details on those interactions rather than for prescriptions from our collaborative procedures or teacher-as-researcher methods.

Thus, this book emerged from the interest expressed by a number of educators who wondered not only about the forms and intentions of our collaboration but also about the stories that we told. Those stories centered on our individual and collective struggles to explicate sources and effects of underlying assumptions that framed our notions of teaching, curriculum, research, and collaboration. Our stories were relayed through descriptions and reflections about our daily interactions with students, with other teachers, with principals and parents. Neither we nor others saw the particulars of our lives as educators as duplicating every teacher's world; rather, they were presented and were received as a mosaic of experiences that provided concrete portrayals of the difficulties and possibilities that teachers encounter when they try to view their work and their knowledges as evolving and creating processes.

I have chosen to tell those stories here as a narrative of collaboration, with much of the detail of our interactions presented through transcribed dialogues of our meetings and excerpts from our writings to one another. The collective narrative contains multiple stories of our shifting relationships to one another, of the difficulties involved in attempting to understand emancipation and empower-ment as possibilities lodged in the daily actions of our teaching, and of the constantly emerging questions that arise from those attempts.

Thus, this narrative contains the stories of our individual struggles within our shared attempt to create collaborative forms of educational inquiry. At the same time, the narrative also is filtered through my experiences of this collective activity. Even as I describe myself as a teacher, I see ways in which my university affiliation automatically highlights the traditional researcher position within our collaborations and within this book as written form of our work together.

However, in openly grappling with the possibility of imposition and in presenting the many voices, the multiple positions and changing perspectives from which each of us speaks, I have tried to point to the ways in which each of us shared in the formation and constant reformation of our collaborative processes. The members of our group participated in the selection of the situations and voices that are presented here. Much of that participation emanated from our realization that each of us, in our long-term collaboration, has changed in many ways. We have begun to hear our multiple voices within the contexts of our sustained collaboration, and thus recognize that "finding voices" is not a definitive event but rather a continuous and relational process.

At the same time, we also believe that teachers' voices, in all their similarities and differences, still are not heard in the clamor for educational reform and in agendas for research on teachers' knowledge. Thus, even as we know that we do not speak from similar positions or from some discovered or fixed stance, we also know that teachers' discussions and reflections on their experiences and their evolving knowledges remain apart from the official perspectives that still regulate and form the conditions for our practice of teaching.

Each of us here is willing to share our stories, then, in the hope that our questions might be heard within the current debates and discussions on educational reform. Although our stories might encourage others to pose their own questions and to create their own versions of our collaborative attempts, the group members have decided that they wish to protect the privacy of those touched by our work. Thus, the group members have chosen to change their names in order to tell their stories and, at the same time, to respect the situations of those with whom they work and interact on a daily basis.

The chronicle begins with my invitation to the five teachers to continue our discussions beyond the confines of the graduate classroom. Chapter One describes the motivations and backgrounds of that invitation, which included our shared experiences of the seminars and texts of graduate studies in curriculum and of qualitative forms of educational research.

Chapter Two provides an introduction to each group member's particular educational situation and to the initial processes by which we attempted to begin our collaborative forms of inquiry. These processes, especially interactive dialogue journal writing, and discussions and reflections on our individual situations within the group context, separate our work from standard forms of educational ethnographies or case studies. Our beginning work together did not include interviews or observations of one another and of our individual educational settings. Rather, our inquiries were centered within the processes by which we attempted to effect collaborative forms of reflection and dialogue, and they focused on our evolving understandings of the forces that guide and shape our daily practice.

Chapter Three delineates the emergence of recurrent obstacles within our collaborative attempts, which we began to construe as constraints in our endeavors. Those obstacles, introduced as themes and variations in this chapter, include time, multiple layers of assumptions and expectations, and uncertainties. Our struggles to see the possibilities for ourselves within these constraints began to emerge as our collaboration extended into a second year.

Our identification of those recurrent obstacles was prelude to the various points of dissonance that erupted within each of us as we continued our collaborative efforts. An episode with a "carton of knowledge" provided a context within which each of us could further grapple with the dissonance that our collaborative intentions and inquiries created. What we called the carton of knowledge actually was a box of files and materials that contained the "prescribed curriculum" for a course that Marjorie, one of the teacher-researchers, was assigned to teach. In Chapter Four, that carton of knowledge is explored as concrete and metaphoric representation of the standard conceptions of knowledge production and research orientations that we were attempting to challenge.

Chapter Five contains further stories of each of the group member's efforts to become challengers in educational worlds that often do not welcome or encourage questions or alternative perspectives. As we debated the benefits and dangers of community, of becoming vocal in our explorations and in our evolving understandings of ourselves as researching teachers, we began to acknowledge the ways in which we challenged and supported one another in our explorations.

As we continue together, beyond the confines of this book, we also are able to begin to view the ways in which our ongoing and long-term collaboration differs from various versions of collaborative research or teacher-as-researcher constructs. Chapter Six explicates those differences, and also points to the strengths and possibilities that we find in our particular versions.

As noted in that chapter, "we're not done yet." Our continuing association affirms the possibilities that we have found thus far in our work together. We invite other classroom and university teachers, school administrators, staff developers, student teachers, teacher educators, and concerned parents and community members to consider the issues and questions that have emerged within our collaboration. We hope that our stories may invite others to join together in creating spaces and finding voices.

Acknowledgments

This book is inspired and formed by the enduring commitment of the five educators who continue to infuse our collaboration with new possibilities.

In turn, our collaborative efforts are supported and nourished by our families and our friends. We gratefully acknowledge those whose understanding and encouragement provide time and spaces for each of us to pursue our questions and our connections.

I especially thank Lois Patton and Alan Tom for their thoughtful and insightful editorial guidance. This written version of our collaboration owes much to the vision and gentle support of these two individuals.

My wish to explore collaborative forms of inquiry emanated from the strength and affirmation shared among a number of colleagues and friends. Conversations with Jean Anyon sparked my initial interest in this work, and her questions and insights enhance both this narrative and our friendship. Incentive, connection, and grounding for my interest in collaboration also emerged through work with Janet Callahan, Carol Clifford, Rosemarie Pace, Mary Lee Martens, Gerry Seifert, Esther Ranells, Georgette Neville Vosseler, and Elizabeth Bauer.

Extended conversations and collaborative work with Ann Berlak and Patti Lather have influenced the form and intentions of this narrative. Encouragement for the sharing of our collaborative journey also emerged through thoughtful responses, suggestions, support and inspiration from Maxine Greene, Jo Anne Pagano, Jean Erdman, Kenny Schiff, Naomi Silverman, Nancy King, Craig Kridel, Alan Block, William Pinar, Donna Petrie, Elizabeth Matthias, Patricia Fonda, Monette Sachs, Ken Kantor, Paul Klohr, Dan Marshall, William

Proefriedt, Elyse Eidman-Aadahl, Carol Alberts, Sylvia Giallombardo, William Paringer, Susan Smith, Kevin Eckstrom, Louise Belcher, Eileen Duffy, Joel Spring, Madeleine Grumet, Jeffrey Gilden, Diane Schwartz, Kay McIntosh, William Schubert, Carol Pope, Sophie Grace, Mrs. Brown, four anonymous readers, and Linda Anderson.

To these people and to my family, I extend my thanks, with affection and gratitude.

CHAPTER ONE

The Invitation

> It is when people become challengers, when they take initiatives, that they begin to create the kinds of spaces where dialogue can take place and freedom can appear. And it is then, and probably only then, that people begin thinking about working together to bring into being a better, fairer, more humane state of things.
>
> —M. Greene, "Reflection and Passion in Teaching"

Sitting at a picnic table on a late summer day in 1986, surrounded by trees that softened the edges of the urban campus, I extended an invitation to the educators who were sharing lunch and conversation with me. I invited them to continue working together, beyond the formal context of our graduate classrooms. Those rooms, with their nailed-down seats and rigid rows, had provided introductory yet limited space for us to effect connections among our varied interests as educators and to study the interrelationships among curriculum, teaching, and research.

These five educators had been students together in several of the graduate classes that I taught on curriculum and on qualitative forms of educational research. As we studied conceptions of curriculum and of research that posed strong challenges and alternatives to the dominant traditions in education, these students raised difficult questions about the possibilities of putting such conceptions to work within the confines of their own classrooms and offices. They even wondered about the extent to which they could ask similar questions in their own educational settings, because they were fairly sure that voicing such alternative possibilities would not be welcomed or

1

encouraged. These students challenged me, then, to consider how these alternatives could become a foundation for their daily teaching and thus contribute to their creation of better, fairer, more humane educational communities.

I share the perspective of those who view curriculum as centered within students' and teachers' biographical, historical, and social relationships. From this perspective, curriculum is created within the relational classroom experiences that individuals share with texts and with one another; at the same time, curriculum also is defined and created by the intersecting forces of existing schooling and social structures. Curriculum research, therefore, encompasses examination of the constantly changing nature of individuals' possibilities within these educational experiences and situations, particularly as they are shaped and reshaped by cultural, political, historical, and gendered dimensions of experience. Political, feminist, poststructuralist, phenomenological, and autobiographical themes distinguish such inquiry (Pinar 1975; 1988).

Such perspectives challenge the dominant traditions in education, including conceptions of curriculum as product, of research as prediction and prescription, of teaching and learning as a series of measurable skills. Yet these educators' experiences in schools coincided with those traditions that regard curriculum as a program of planned activities on specific subject area content, and research as analysis of quantitative data derived from experimental and quasi-experimental designs. These linear and rather specific interpretations are referred to as empirical-analytic, or positivist, and they remain dominant perspectives in educational research and practice.

In our classes, I had juxtaposed these standard perspectives with curricular and research orientations that called into question the concepts of neutrality, objectivity, observable facts, transparent description, clean separation of the interpreter and the interpreted that are basic to positivist ways of knowing (Lather 1989b). We examined aspects of the hidden or implicit curriculum that, through organization of time, knowledge, students, and instruction, quietly reinforced established social structures, positions of authority, and linear, determined ways of knowing within schools. We began to connect the technical and efficient agendas of positivist orientations with the closing rather than the opening of spaces, and we began to question what we could do, in our teaching and our research, to create spaces between ourselves and what enveloped and surrounded us.

As we explored curriculum and research perspectives and approaches that challenged these positivist conceptions, students voiced conflicts that the unfamiliar perspectives created for them. They were drawn to the possibilities that seemed inherent in these alternative positions: teachers, with their colleagues and with their students, might be able to work together in ways that would encourage conceptions of themselves as challengers and creators rather than just transmitters and receivers of others' constructions of knowledge. However, none of us had been prepared, either as students or now as educators, to consider ourselves as participants or creators in teaching, research, and curricular processes and constructions.

Therefore, such possibilities also elicited anxious yet intrigued inquiries among the educators who were studying curriculum and research from these new angles. What was entailed in creating and working in "the kinds of spaces where dialogue can take place and freedom can appear?" What could we do about our frustrations that constantly emerged in our attempts to find or to create such spaces within our classrooms, already cramped with curriculum mandates and validated versions of testable knowledge? Who would want to create or to inhabit such spaces with us? What would happen to our existing educational relationships and to our conceptions and expectations of ourselves, if we were to engage in such inquiries? How could we work to change the technical conceptions of teaching, research, and curriculum that were so prevalent in our lives, that seemed to thwart our active and creative participation, and yet seemed to receive such support, especially in terms of performance and evaluation criteria, from the institutions in which we worked?

Such questions, framed by these educators' concerns as well as my own, finally impelled me to invite these five students to move beyond our stiff classroom, with its raised platform and lectern, upon and behind which I could never stand. We clearly had identified, throughout our class discussions and studies, an interest in wanting to puzzle together about the difficulties as well as possibilities for ourselves and others that seemed inherent within these alternative perspectives. The five teachers especially had expressed interest in and curiosity about the possibilities of examining these perspectives by assuming the stance of teacher-researchers, and we had begun to explore the dimensions of that concept in the closing sessions of our course in qualitative research. However, as we talked and laughed together on that summer day, we were not conscious of the spaces that we had begun to create. We only knew that we were reluctant to end our final class together, and so we lingered over our impromptu picnic, talking of possible ways in which we might extend our conversations and explore our questions.

Beginnings

These individuals, although sharing the role of graduate student, represented a wide range of educational experiences and positions: at that time, Katherine was a first-grade teacher with eight years of teaching experience; Cheryl was an elementary special education teacher with five years of experience in self-contained classrooms as well as in resource-room settings; Beth was a junior high school math teacher with eighteen years of teaching experience; Marjorie was a high-school science teacher with seventeen years of teaching experience at the elementary, junior high, and high school levels; Kevin had completed five years as a school psychologist, after serving five years as a high school theology teacher. I was finishing my seventh year as a university teacher, having previously taught high school English for seven years.

The settings in which these elementary and high school educators worked, although similar in function, often were more constricted than mine, given the length of the teaching day and the numbers of students with whom they interacted. One issue that compelled us was the extent to which our varying educational environments constricted possibilities for teachers and students to become challengers. Although my schedule would indicate more flexibility of time, thus perhaps leading to more opportunities for such explorations, I shared in these students' feelings of isolation and restriction within predominant and accepted forms of research and teaching. We all felt that we worked within educational environments and structures that often closed rather than opened the psychic and physical space deemed necessary for critical dialogue and humane action.

My invitation as well as these teachers' acceptance of that invitation emerged, in part, then, from our various experiences of isolation, confusion, and frustration in our educational settings. As well, we were drawn together by our interests in attempting to enact the forms and intentions of curricular and research orientations that moved beyond the boundaries of prediction and control. Although these educators had expressed frustrations with the ways in which behavioral objectives and predetermined outcomes of learning activities, for example, limited their own sense of participation and ownership in curriculum and teaching endeavors, they also expressed confusion about how they might become creators and challengers within teaching, curriculum, and research agendas and approaches that seemed fixed and immutable.

Thus, these educators expressed great interest in wanting to explore what it might mean to try to teach and dialogue with others in a freedom-producing way, while, at the same time, to cover a sick colleague's lunch duty and grade papers before the next class. We all wanted to share explorations of what "emancipation" and "empowerment" and "critical pedagogy" might mean to those who faced the closing of spaces each day, in classrooms filled with children, in guidance offices filled with computer printouts of these childrens' school lives, in principals' and evaluators' offices filled with the schedules of others. We gathered together, in part then, because we agreed that

> We have to find out how to open such spheres, such spaces, where a better state of things can be imagined; because it is only through the projection of a better social order that we can perceive the gaps in what exists and try to transform and repair. . . . As teachers learning along with those we try to provoke to learn, we may be able to inspire hitherto unheard voices . . . to break through the opaqueness, to refuse the silences. (Greene 1986a, 441)

My wish to continue working with these five graduate students–educators reflected my own struggles with the enactment of these conceptualizations of teaching, curriculum, and research in academic settings that rewarded excellence in terms of quantified concepts of productivity. As well, my desire to research these alternative possibilities with classroom teachers reflected my growing conviction that the importance of these reconceptualized perspectives might be obscured if they only were examined within the confines of graduate classrooms and theoretical discourse. I felt a strong need to respond to calls for portrayals of concrete situations in which teachers grappled with contradictions and constraints that inhibited or blurred their desires to participate in the reciprocity of dialogue and action. Such reciprocity undergirded concepts, such as "empowerment" and "emancipatory pedagogy and research," that were emerging especially from these alternative perspectives; and yet I thought these often remained abstracted from teachers' daily lives, muffled by the clamor of students' voices in the halls during the change of classes and the faceless voice of the public address system announcer, calling for attendance slips to be forwarded to the front office.

I wanted to talk and to debate with these educators as we all attempted to act on the obstacles as well as the possibilities that we saw lurking within these conceptions. I, too, felt that sometimes those possibilities remained separated from our daily lives, stashed as theory against the shelves of our studies. The obstacles were the "real part," as these students had said, and were the impetus for the constant questions that eventually resulted in my invitation to join together.

The Nature of Our Narratives

This book is a chronicle of nearly three years of meeting, discussion, reflection, and action by six educators who wanted to push beyond the separations of isolated graduate student–classroom teacher–professor stances, and to extend the studies that we had begun together in graduate education courses in curriculum theory and research. Our narratives detail our attempts to become teacher-researchers as well as our efforts to research forms of collaboration that could enhance our understandings of ourselves as challengers. To become researching teachers required that we look beneath the rhetorics of "effective teaching" and school "reform" as well as "empowering pedagogies" and "emancipatory research" in order to dig into the possibilities and limitations that these various perspectives hold for our daily teaching lives and for working together to build just and humane educational communities.

As such, this chronicle also is incomplete. Because we continue to meet as a collaborative group beyond the time and context of these written words, we can provide no definitive answers for the forms that teacher-oriented research, or curriculum as lived experience, or critical and reflective pedagogy, for example, might take, or for the spaces that such perspectives might require or create. What we can offer is a detailing of the processes as well as problematic aspects of dialogue and collaboration that characterize our particular forms of inquiry; we can share the constantly emerging and changing nature of our voices, and of the questions and points of dissonance that accompany our explorations. We also want to share the strengths and support that we derive from our work together, and the ways in which our collaborative inquiry has changed the forms and intentions of our daily educational endeavors.

Thus, our narratives reflect individual questions, perspectives, areas of dissonance and dissatisfaction; they are woven together by the threads of our similarities and our differences as we attempt to understand and to act upon our own possibilities and upon our commitments to the creation of spaces where voices can be raised within and across the differences that divide us.

In a sense, then, the larger chronicle is a narrative of community. This narrative is rooted in the processes of educational life in its everyday aspects and is episodic, built primarily around the continuous small-scale negotiations and daily procedures through which we sustain our interactions (Zagarell 1988). In discussing our interdependence, however, we also point to the ways in which our differences as well as our similarities contribute to our understandings of collaboration and of ourselves as constantly changing contributors to this evolving community.

Our narrative of community thus contains multiple accounts of our individual and collective processes as we work to become challengers in our educational contexts. These multiple episodes are one way of challenging the ahistorical and essentialized selves that our stories tend to create; they are one way to diminish the coherence and logical development with which we tend to infuse the stories that we tell (Grumet 1987). Our multiple narratives also "cultivate our capacity to see through the outer forms, the habitual explanation of things, the stories we tell in order to keep others at a distance" (Pinar 1988, 149).

Thus, our narratives, here told through transcribed tape-recordings of our meetings and excerpts from dialogue journal writing, are filled with the words and writings of all the group

7

members. These stories represent attempts by each of us to see through habitual explanations, including our tendencies to reject others' narratives that do not correspond to our experiences of our educational worlds or to our established positions within them (Brodkey 1989).

Much of my struggle throughout our collective narrative involves my attempts to recognize and to avoid the possible convolutions, misrepresentations, and impositions of the interpretive authorial voice embedded within my established position as initiator of the invitation. As I shared this struggle with the group members, we all became involved in attempting to develop ways in which to acknowledge each of our varying positions and situations, while at the same time attempting to explicate and honor our own (Berlak 1988). In many ways, our narrative of community exemplifies the struggles of position and voice in collaborations among university and classroom teachers. It also exemplifies a major tension among academic research communities in terms of appropriate researcher stance in relation to "subjects," data, and the possibilities of interpretation. By situating all of our collaborative experiences as the center of our inquiry, I have tried to confront and to disrupt the possibilities of overvaluing my role as the individual "in charge" of our research efforts (Patai 1988).

I think that my particular struggle over these issues represents constant tension; on the one hand there is my fear of imposing an assumption of "authoritative discourse which disallows the possibility for the students to 'tell' their own stories, and to present and then question the experiences they bring into play" (Giroux 1988, 256). On the other hand there is my growing understanding that "the female professor is a strange creature—neither father nor mother." (Pagano 1988a, 523).

I participate in feminist curricularists' search for ways in which to speak in voices that do not replicate dominant discursive practices or the unequal class, race, and gender relationships often embedded within those practices. As I reflect upon the impetus for my invitation to the five graduate students, I acknowledge that my desire for community and for the spaces in which educators might study and talk together emerged through this search, as well as through a concurrent struggle. I am still grappling with the sense that there need be no conflict between nurturance and authority, between the private and the public, as long as we can acknowledge the requirements of affiliation, thus tempering our need for proof:

> For even as I sit alone in my room, I feel a demand upon my attention that necessarily attaches me to the world. Our intellectual work ought to give point to and signify those attachments. Our attachments ought to give point to our work. (Pagano 1988a, 527)

My fear of imposing myself on our collaborative inquiry emanated from my position as university teacher and thus "expert" according to many traditional conceptions of university-school collaborative projects, as originator of the invitation, and as framer of the initial strands of inquiry that led to our collective studies. Clearly, my desire to acknowledge the attachments that gave point to my work, and my continuing struggle to understand the basis of my own authority as woman teacher enabled me to at least begin to see that my fears of imposing were situated within structures that often necessitate and reinforce "authoritative discourse." My invitation was my own initial step in challenging these structures and the distances that they mandated between teachers and students, and in searching for ways to speak that emanated from my own experiences of those distances.

However, my invitation alone did not dispel the fear or the expectations that it signified; we all struggled with the group members' initial acceptance of and expectations for my role as leader, with my resistance to that role, and with the changing relationships among us as we worked to make explicit both our positions and our attachments.

Our tensions surrounding these struggles are major themes throughout our narratives. Because of our continuing efforts to address these issues and to "interrupt the assumption of unchanging, irreversible, and asymmetrical social and political relations between the privileged and unprivileged subjects represented in a particular discourse" (Brodkey 1989, 127), I wish to acknowledge here the incomplete nature of this chronicle, as well as to present, as fully as possible, the interrupting, reflective, and challenging voices of our collaboration. As members of the group remind me, they chose to accept the invitation, and they are actively involved in the creation of our processes of collaboration and dialogue. They have stood at the computer screen to add and delete words, and have suggested examples that they felt might further illuminate our exchanges. Through our writings and our discussions, through the reading and rereading of our resulting narratives, all members of our collaborative group have participated in the creation of this chronicle.

Still, this book can present only parts of our individual and collective stories. By sharing our collaborative efforts and by voicing the differences among our experiences of that process, we also attempt to refer to some of the complexity of experience that any story necessarily reduces (Brodkey 1987).

As Grumet too reminds us, although our stories come from us, we cannot be reduced to them. However, in the telling, we may diminish the distance between the private and public poles of our experience:

> As we study the forms of our own experience, not only are we searching for evidence of the external forces that have diminished us; we are also recovering our own possibilities. We work to remember, imagine, and realize ways of knowing and being that can span the chasm presently separating our public and private worlds. (Grumet 1988a, xv)

This narrative, then, attempts to bring teachers' voices to the center of the dialogue and debate surrounding current educational reform, teacher education restructuring efforts, and research on teachers' knowledge. Our group's explorations of the possibilities of collaborative and interactive research as one way in which we might "recover our own possibilities" are at the heart of this chronicle. The stories here reveal knowledge that often conflicts with, or is not reflected in, the dominant stories (Harding 1987) that educational culture tells about its teachers, its students, its research orientations, and its effective reforms. Among the possibilities that we may recover in the telling of our stories here, however, is the hope that, by knowing the ways of others' histories, we may be encouraged to see beyond and through our own (deLauretis 1986).

The Background of the Invitation

My invitation to these teachers obviously had part of its origins in my teaching, research, and in-service activities; as well, my invitation was encouraged by these educators' interest and points of inquiry about the perspectives that I presented in our graduate classes together. Here, I wish to briefly sketch those points and counterpoints; our text then reveals their intersections and contradictions as well as group members' individual and collective points of dissonance and agreement.

I teach curriculum theory from perspectives that challenge the limitations of the dominant conception of curriculum as course of study, as product, as text to be covered, and ends to be achieved and measured. I know that these conceptions are part of what constitute working definitions of curriculum, especially for teachers and administrators in schools. However, as I have noted, my work is aligned with those who view curriculum as also defined within students' and teachers' biographical, historical, and social situations that they bring to the classroom as well as within the relational classroom experiences that they share with texts, with education structures, and with one another.

In challenging the managerial and technical conceptions of cur-riculum as a packaged and predetermined program, curriculum the-orists who place persons at the center of the schooling situation also reject the function of theory as simply knowing possible problems and solutions in order to anticipate and control their outcomes.

> Curriculum theory seeks to restore the contemplative moment in which we interrupt our taken-for-granted understandings of our work, and ask again the basic questions practical activity silences. . . . Just as what we think and know about our work is contradicted daily by the events in which we participate, the actual experience of teaching and the certainties that activity offers may be undermined by the questions and alternatives that theory cultivates. (Pinar and Grumet 1988, 99)

To interrupt the "taken-for-granted understandings" of our daily work as teachers, to turn our "practical" understandings of curriculum and teaching to the underside of theory, requires, I believe, both space and a research orientation to our work.

> To be oriented as researchers or theorists means that we do not separate theory from life, the public from the private. We are not simply being pedagogues here and researchers there—we are researchers oriented to the world in a pedagogic way. (van Manen 1988, 450)

I had been grappling with my own constraints as a woman aca-demic who taught, theorized, and researched those forms of curriculum inquiry that were considered alternative in my institutional set-ting, which favored more traditional definitions of appropriate knowledge production and dissemination. I felt the marginalization of my perspectives, in a setting that still offered relative space, if not support, in which to pursue my academic interests. Given my own feelings of constraint, I worried that classroom teachers had even less time and supportive context in which to challenge prevailing yet lim-ited conceptions of curriculum, teaching, and research. I shared the concerns of others in education who worried that the current push for "excellence" shoved classroom teachers to the borders of reform ef-forts, thus constricting even further the room in which they might work with students and with one another in interactive and relational ways, and in which they might conceive of such interactions as forms of more challenging curriculum and research.

My own feelings of disjuncture within the university had led me to consider the multiple perspectives of those who wished to challenge existing oppressive situations and static forms of curriculum, teaching, and research, and to develop new ways of working; the goal of these critiques and methodological considerations included not only the revelation but also the change of oppressive contexts and structures. As I explored these perspectives and approaches, I listened for teachers' voices as they recounted their attempts to become challengers within bureaucratic and personal systems that did not encourage such action. I heard these alternative voices in the work of curriculum theorists, feminist scholars, and writing process researchers who chose autobiographical and self-reflexive ways of situating themselves and the teachers with whom they worked within the various contexts that they sought to critique, to research, and to make more humane.

Through modes in which teachers might examine their own situations and the nature of their positions in schooling and social systems, these approaches offered possibilities that the examined yet unreified teacher's voice, the researching teacher herself, could be included in the discussions of educational reform, of teacher empowerment, of possibilities for practitioners who wished to become reflective as well as active agents in the construction of a more humane world.

The research orientations that align with these views of curriculum and teaching are those that fall under the generic term, *qualitative* research. Some argue for the terms *naturalistic, interpretive, interactive,* or *ethnographic* as appropriate for these forms of research; my concern is not to debate the labels under which our collaborative work might fall, but rather to point to the challenges to technical and positivist conceptions of curriculum, teaching, and research that such orientations provide.

Positivist research includes goals of prediction, control, and generalization within a quantitative tradition based on the idea of an independently existing social reality that can be described as it really is (Smith and Heshusius 1986). In contrast, qualitative research, although reflecting a diversity of traditions and methodologies, is rooted in a phenomenological paradigm which holds that reality is socially constructed through individual or collective definitions of the situation (Firestone 1987). This research, in general, aims to be:

> empirical without being positivist; to be rigorous and systematic in investigating the slippery phenomenon of everyday interaction and its connections, through the medium of subjective meaning, with the wider social world. (Erickson 1986, 120)

One orientation within which some curricularists work attempts to extend the researcher role into interactive and relational forms. The qualitative researcher becomes not only "immersed in the phenomenon of interest" (Powdermaker 1966) but also attempts to make explicit her intentions within the research effort and to acknowledge the ways in which those intentions order the theoretical direction of the discourse beyond the narrative (Sullivan, Martinic, and Walker 1987).

Through autobiographical and self-reflexive methods that focus on how we construct the very examination of our teaching and research processes, some curricularists attempt to carry out research as a form of *praxis* (Lather 1986), an encompassing of both reflection and action as a form of inquiry that promotes "a better, fairer, more humane" world. This approach to research attempts to be a democratized process of inquiry characterized by negotiation and reciprocity among the researcher and the researched; it places the shifting interactions, expectations, and subjectivities of both the researcher and the researched at the heart of the inquiry. Such a research orientation necessarily includes a willingness by all involved to risk and to be changed by the research process itself:

13

> Once the subjects enter into inquiry, the distinction traditionally maintained between them and researchers collapses and both become knowers. This change in turn requires us to redefine knowers as people who understand and learn, whether or not in academic modes. (Messer-Davidow 1985, 17)

A further goal of such a research orientation is to develop theory democratically, as a collective effort among the researcher and the research subjects. Such research

> is less likely to generate propositions that are imposed by the researcher and more likely to be responsive to the logic of evidence that does not fit the researcher's preconceptions . . . and encourages the research subjects' empowerment through systematic reflection upon their own situations and roles in reproducing or transforming existing power relations. (Roman and Apple 1988, 38)

Thus, the researchers and the researched wish not only to describe and analyze social practices, but also to interrupt those social practices that most often oppress certain designated classes within educational institutions, namely students, teachers, minorities, and women (Brodkey 1987).

To do this, however, requires that we also examine the ways in which our very research processes might unintentionally reproduce those same oppressions by imposing meanings on situations, rather than constructing meaning through negotiation with research participants. Thus, we must question our very conceptions of "knowing," from both researcher and participant positions:

> What would it mean to recognize not only that a multiplicity of knowledges are present . . . as a result of the way difference has been used to structure social relations inside and outside the classroom, but that these knowledges are contradictory, partial, and irreducible? . . . What kind of educational project could redefine "knowing" so that it no longer describes the activities of those in power . . . ? What kind of educational project would redefine the silence of the unknowable, . . . and make of that silence "a language of its own" that changes the nature and direction of speech itself? (Ellsworth 1989, 321)

Questions such as these force us all to confront tendencies to simplify the world into subject and other, tendencies to assume or to determine which objects, nature, and "others" are to be known or are ultimately knowable at a level of determination never accorded to the

Cooperation etc

"knower" himself or herself (Ellsworth 1989). Questions such as these encourage us to "acknowledge the authority and creativity of the speaker weaving her own text" (Patai 1988), and to constantly challenge the ways in which our research processes, even if described as reciprocal and liberating in intent, still might contribute to positions of power in which the researcher alone remains the origin of what can be known and of what should be done (Ellsworth 1989).

These perspectives are significant for the educational research community's renewed interest in the emancipatory potentials of action research and the teacher-as-researcher:

> In emancipatory action research, the critical group takes responsibility for developing practice and understanding, viewing these as socially constructed within the interactive dynamic of curriculum life. Emancipation counts as the empowerment of the research group in its quest for a more just, rational, and democratic curriculum. . . . A goal is to allow the group to take charge of decision-making about curriculum matters—about which problems to study, how to study them, and what changes to implement as a result of inquiry. . . . Practitioners are free to exercise their critical perspectives and assume control over knowledge and curriculum, not to function as the servants of authority. (McKernan 1988, 193)

Part of my invitation to the teachers had emerged through my questions about whether emancipatory concepts of teacher-as-researcher were possible within the enclosed spaces of prevailing schooling structures and functions. Further, I wondered if these concepts even were desirable as goals in teachers' research, given the "authoritative discourse" that I felt often undergirded such terms as "empowerment" and "emancipation," especially when they were presented as someone else's conceptualization, authorization, or transmission of power or decision-making skills to teachers and students.

These words were not the ones that teachers most often used to describe the conditions and situations in which they wished to teach. More often, it seemed to me, teachers spoke of caring about kids, of wanting to help them in their struggles to grow and to learn. They also spoke about wanting opportunities for themselves to develop as teachers; they did not see these opportunities in the perfunctory tasks they performed as classroom managers. Teachers spoke of the daily infringements upon their practice that often came, for example,

15

in the form of "pull-out" programs and "add-ons" to the curriculum. And, if I asked them, in graduate classrooms or in in-service settings, to dream out loud about their ideal educational worlds, they spoke of longing for more time and bigger spaces and fewer numbers of students in their classes so that they could, as one teacher said, "touch each one." These were personal words, the words of teachers who worked in daily situations in which the notions as well as the language of "empowerment" and "emancipation" seemed distant, even foreign, to their lives. And although their words alluded to the problems that concepts of "teacher empowerment and emancipation" wished to address, teachers often spoke of their discomfort with those terms. "Who will get to empower us?", one of these students asked. "And what if we don't want it?", another replied.

Working in an in-service setting with teachers who wished to incorporate the writing process into their classrooms had provided me with introductory perspectives for the teacher-as-researcher. I also had the opportunity to ponder the applicability, as well as possible meanings, of emancipatory conceptions within this approach.

The writing process movement has contributed to the concept of teacher-as-researcher as a viable and visible way through which to increase our understandings of the role of writing in the learning process (Myers 1985) as well as to acknowledge the "quiet form of research" (Britton 1987) that is inherent within teachers' practice. Many writing researchers, focusing on the roles of response, voice, and community in the teaching and learning of the writing process (Berthoff 1987a; Freedman 1985; Heath and Branscombe 1985), argue that teachers must be actively involved in interpreting as well as conducting their own research (Florio-Ruane and Dohanich 1984) in order to "reclaim their classrooms" (Goswami and Stillman 1987).

These perspectives warn against forms of teacher-as-researcher that simply replicate the procedures and intentions of prevailing positivist norms in educational research. These norms serve only to initiate teachers into the dominant research paradigm and its accompanying language, methodologies, and detached researcher stance (May 1982).

Further, notions of teacher–researcher collaboration often reinforce the "expert" status of those who enter classrooms to determine as well as to guide teachers' research activities. Much of this work appears to serve the primary researchers' interests or to focus upon teachers' sense of efficacy in terms of students' raised achievement scores. Although appearing to lean in the direction of possible teacher inclusion as co-researcher by acknowledging the contextual complexities of teachers' work (Ashton and Webb 1986), much of this research still excludes teachers from participation in determining research focus or interpretation. Implied in this arrangement is the belief that efforts to make researchers out of teachers will somehow violate or negate the expertise that each has to offer (Applebee 1987), thus reinforcing the secondary role that teachers play in the generation of knowledge about their own work.

As I worked with teachers in the in-service setting, then, I kept searching for conceptualizations of the teacher as the researcher of her own underlying assumptions, as connected to her particular biographical, cultural, and historical situations, and as manifested in her classroom processes and interactions. Through the effects of participants upon one another, upon the research process, and upon the contexts in which they worked, I looked for collaborative approaches that recognized the capacities of educators to challenge and to change existing situations that limited their students as well as themselves.

By trying to place teachers, rather than myself, at the center of their own research processes within our in-service contexts, I began to see ways in which I might refocus my understanding of current approaches to research on teachers' knowledge. Teachers who conducted research within their classroom contexts were beginning to examine not only teaching—learning situations but also their own conceptions of their knowledge and practice. I thought that these perspectives could at least call attention to the chasm that separates what outside researchers produce as reconstructions of teachers' knowledge, even when this research is conducted from a "teacher's perspective" (Clandinin 1986; Elbaz 1983; Perl and Wilson 1986), and what teachers consider to be their knowledges (Elbaz 1987).

These perspectives perhaps also could challenge the work of those who wished to "empower" teachers without questioning the authority from which they granted empowerment or considering teachers' own conceptions of what might constitute empowerment for themselves. I believed these teacher-centered perspectives on research, teaching, and curriculum questioned the simple addition of unexamined teachers' perspectives to the reform debates and to plans for the restructuring of schools and teacher preparation programs as sufficient for "teacher empowerment."

This additive strategy had proven insufficient, for example, in feminists' struggles to examine as well as to challenge the structures of the disciplines, of the academy, and of conceptions of knowledge production. By posing gender analysis as problematic, that is, by questioning the simple addition of unexamined women's perspectives as sufficient for changing structures and expectations, feminist scholars have pointed to the necessity of varied analyses of the multiple perspectives and experiences of women (Harding 1986; Tabakin and Densmore 1986). Such questioning pointed, I thought, to the need for similar self-reflexive analyses and critiques by teachers who wished to examine their own expectations and assumptions within the social and political intersections of current educational reform.

Therefore, in working to explore the dimensions and intersections of these various points of inquiry, I shared the goals of those who sought emancipatory knowledge that

> increases awareness of the contradictions hidden or distorted by everyday understandings, and in doing so, . . . directs attention to the possibilities for social transformation inherent in the present configuration of social processes. (Lather 1986, 259)

I agreed that there were necessary struggles inherent in individuals' attempts not to impose the concept of "empowerment" upon others in the name of liberation. I found profound examples of that understanding of the delicate and potentially dangerous nature of the empowered position and voice among feminist scholars who, although working from a variety of perspectives, constantly raise questions about who can be a "knower" and have a voice.

By acknowledging that individuals' experiences differ by race, class, gender, and culture, feminists also point to the fact that "empowerment" is located within the reciprocity of relationships and lodged in the personal spaces of people's daily lives. It is in this sense that we cannot separate "theory from life, the public from the private."

> Empowerment endures, i.e., people continue to feel empowered when their collective struggles result in fundamental alterations in social hierarchies

that are experienced on a day-to-day basis as an improvement in the quality of life. (Radford-Hill 1986, 159)

Forming the Questions

These, then, were the currents of thought that I had shared with these students in our graduate classrooms. My own struggles and questions with these issues and perspectives, combined with these educators' questions, had compelled my invitation.

Clearly, my work with teachers in graduate classroom and in-service settings was focused upon alternative conceptions of curriculum and teaching, and I had expressed my commitment to the creation of *praxis*-oriented research approaches. However, the actual possibility that, given their literal and metaphoric lack of space, classroom teachers could combine such perceptions and commitments, and experience, on a day-to-day basis, an improvement in the quality of their lives appeared problematic to me. I argued for the more liberating effect of teachers conducting research within their own classrooms as one way in which they might better understand their roles as creators and not just dispensers of knowledge; and yet I was unsure of the ways in which such processes might truly transcend the traditional conceptions of research, teaching, and curriculum that permeated my own as well as these teachers' lives.

The questions that the teachers themselves raised for me focused upon those very limitations. They wanted to explore and reflect on their roles as agents in the construction and interpretation of knowledge, and on the social structures and power relationships that often influence who and what can count as "knowers" and "the known". They wanted to draw on their experiences as a way to value their personal knowledge, to reflect on their knowing-in-action (Schön 1983), and to see individual intentions as constructed within particular historical and social realities. However, these teachers also brought countless examples from their teaching experiences and situations, as well as from their own constructions and expectations for themselves as teachers, which they felt constrained the pursuit and development of these alternative perspectives as ways of creating a "better, fairer, more humane state of things."

Thus, we were drawn together finally by our questions. We knew that the questions differed, depending upon our particular situations, but we also felt that our questions intersected enough to warrant a collaborative approach to our investigations. None of us was able, at that picnic lunch, to articulate these questions in any systematic way, and we continue, beyond the boundaries of this narrative, to explore and to debate the questions that initiated our collaboration, as well as those that have emerged from our collective inquiries. These questions were not formed in any coherent way as we began our collaboration, and yet they existed as vague promptings that allowed us to gather and begin to articulate them as guideposts for our evolving work. Thus, these question that, in unformed ways, precipitated our initial gathering together are ones that compel us still:

- What are the links between personal and social change? How can teachers become challengers not only of their individually constructed assumptions but also of the larger social and political contexts that frame and often shape their work? What are the internal and external inhibitors to teachers' attempts to become challengers?

- What does it mean to do our questioning in a collaborative fashion? If we agree upon the necessity of thinking and acting in critical ways as requisite for transforming the nature and relationships of teaching and research as well as for transforming teachers' "institutionally infantilized" roles (Erickson 1986), then what role does collaborative investigation play in this transformative venture? How might we work toward "collaborative inquiry" (Oakes, Hare and Sirotnik 1986) that includes a democratic approach that is equitable and consensual rather than merely participatory? In what ways may we support one another and in what ways might we hinder one another as we search for the communities of which Greene (1986) and Freire (1985) and other speak as they detail various visions of teachers as empowered individuals who work together to create a more humane world?

- What are the relationships between and among reflection and action, teaching and research, individual emancipation and collective emancipation? If we begin to examine our underlying assumptions as part of a larger study of pedagogy and research, what is the nature of the movement between our individual understandings and the collective understandings that evolve from the questioning process? What does it mean to move in and out of the particular and the general, to move between and among self-reflexivity and the interactive reflexivity within a group?

- Related to these questions are those created by interactive and *praxis*-oriented research approaches. In what ways are the evolving studies of ourselves as teacher-researchers illustrative of both the particular and the generalizable in studies of teaching? What meanings do our explorations have beyond the confines of our idiosyncratic questions and contexts? In what ways may our descriptions of the problems and possibilities of becoming "challengers" illuminate the processes as well as impediments for others? In what ways do our questions and explorations reflect the concerns and issues of others working within educational contexts? What issues of imposition, including representations of language and voice, might our work address?

- If we view our teaching as a form of research, and if we see ways in which our own researching can inform our teaching as well as empower our roles within the educational community and society, then what changes must we address in our personal and professional constructs of teaching and research, and the relationships inherent within those constructs?

- What roles do writing and dialogue play in the examination of these questions, of ourselves, and of our relationships to the contexts and structures in which we teach, research, counsel and administer? How might our questions about these very processes enable us "to break with submergence, to transform" (Greene 1986a, 429)?

Thus, as these students accepted my invitation to continue our explorations, and as we ended our picnic lunch, we spoke in generalities about the outlines of our work, and not in the specifics of these questions. However, we had begun a collaboration that has expanded into spaces that none of us could have imagined on that hot summer day.

CHAPTER TWO

Creating Spaces

O ur research group began meeting in September 1986. Although we had discussed possible directions for our collaboration at that summer picnic, we had few ideas about how to become instant "challengers." A major tension in exploring emancipatory possibilities of ourselves as teachers-researchers was how to focus on interactions within the classroom, the counseling cubicle, or the chairperson's office without losing sight of the larger world.

Through the collaborative aspects of our investigations, we slowly began to find the connections between our examinations of ourselves and the often controlling forces of the social and cultural contexts in which we worked; it was through our interactions that we began to see the blurring of the distances between our public and private worlds. However, we only began to understand our reciprocal and often changing connections to these contexts by placing ourselves and our interrelationships at their center.

Approaches to Our Studies

During our first meeting in September, we set the general parameters of our work together, and those procedures still constitute the context within which we continue our dialogues and explorations. We meet as a group an average of once a month, and

23

during those two- to three-hour sessions, we discuss emergent questions and unexpected connections, contradictions, and points of dissonance in our evolving collaboration and in our attempts to become challenging, researching teachers.

We never have set an agenda for this collective space, although in our initial meetings, we tended to "go around the room" in order to hear what each person was doing or considering as part of his or her research. This pattern has dissolved, and now the dialogue often continues as an extension of the last session's questions, or in response to a participant's reaction to events or feelings inspired by our work, or as a reflection of the group's questions about the very processes of our collaboration.

In our first meeting, I did reiterate my interest in exploring the emancipatory possibilities of teacher-as-researcher, but I then posited that suggestion as problematic. I tried to explain the underlying assumptions that gave impetus to my invitation, and yet I felt anxious that I could guarantee neither the forms nor the directions of our work (from a tape-recorded transcription of our September 20, 1986, meeting):

> I don't know if teachers engaging in research would feel that as possibly liberating. I don't even know how teachers would want to define liberation for themselves. I do know that the teachers I work with in schools and in our classes voice a lot of frustrations and feelings of impotence in terms of schooling decisions and activities. So that's my hunch about teacher-as-researcher—that something would happen in terms of how you see yourself and act as teacher and in how you relate to your students and your school's structures. And then if you combine it with this group thing, this collaborative support, then I think a lot more things could happen. But I don't know what. That's why I want to do this.
>
> My theoretical assumptions—you know this by now—include rejection of deficit models of staff development and approaches to research and teaching that determine teachers' deficiencies and then tell them how to fix themselves, or how and what to teach. Those deficit models convince me that teacher-as-researcher could be a possibly "empowering" kind of process, to use that current key word. I think our investigations could begin to give us our voices.
>
> That's the best framing I can come up with right now that would move us beyond teacher-as-researcher as simply initiation into the dominant research modes. I want us to be at the center of our teaching and research.

Since none of us was sure of the forms that "emancipatory research and pedagogy" might take, other than trying to place ourselves at the center of those processes, the group members pointed to research possibilities within their own classrooms or other educational contexts as beginning points. As such, these foci conformed to standard teacher-as-researcher approaches, and the group members were comfortable with picking "external" focal points with which to begin their explorations. We did not discuss the nature of our conceptions of research beyond my introductory statements at this session. It is only within the unfolding of our discussions that we actually have begun to scrutinize the relationships among various conceptions of teaching and research, to examine the difficulties and dangers of imposing ourselves on the center of those processes, and to note the changes in our conceptions of those relationships that continue to emerge throughout our collaborative endeavors.

The teachers raised many questions in that first session about possible approaches to their individual research interests. Beth, influenced by some journal articles about teacher-as-researcher, asked if we were going to bring topics to the group and then pick the top one or two for collaborative investigations. Beth continued:

> As soon as I said that, I knew that isn't what I wanted to do. But is there a right way to go about this? I'm afraid that there is, but, at the same time, I'd like to get started and see what happens. Is that O.K.?

Beth's hesitancy reflected the group's feelings, even as we continued to work through possible procedures and directions during that first meeting. Marjorie spoke of feeling "all over the place" in terms of her particular research approaches; Kevin said he wasn't sure whether to "broaden or narrow" his research ideas in order to get going; and I quite often said in that first session, "I don't know."

What I was able to say, at that first meeting, was that I wanted the focus of my research within this joint venture to include the processes and limitations of our collaboration. I wanted to research the varied aspects of teacher-as-researcher constructs that might enhance as well as limit our processes of collaborative inquiry. I wanted to explore dimensions of teachers' knowledges, including my own, from within the vantage points of our own researching efforts, and to consider myself and these five teachers as subjects as well as conductors of our own research. This relocation of the traditional researcher stance from outside to inside the "subjects' spaces" thus would redirect my research focus from the teachers' classroom research and their findings, which was a typical university researcher's perspective, to the processes of our collaboration.

Further, as part of my attempt to work out some of the interactive aspects suggested by emancipatory research approaches, I proposed that we keep journals as yet another space for dialogue to take place. The teachers agreed that they would engage in dialogue journal writing with me; that is, we would write back and forth to one another about whatever issues emerged in our individual and collective inquiries. The five also wanted, however, to hold the option of journal writing as a private and individual activity (Holly 1989), thus adding another dimension to our research.

I specifically proposed dialogue journal writing because of its potential congruence with emancipatory conceptions of teaching and research. Curriculum and writing researchers recently have focused upon the benefits of the interactive, functional, and self-generated written conversations between teachers and students (Roderick 1986; Roderick and Berman 1984; Shuy 1987; Staton 1980); the interactive format of conversation and equal turns on the same topics in dialogue journal writing is different from traditional student journals. In those, teachers might make a marginal comment, or might not respond at all, even preferring that students write for a certain number of minutes per class session. In contrast, the goal of dialogue journal writing is to carry on a discussion about some important topic over several days, within a classroom context, or over several weeks or months, within a collaborative context such as our research group. Researchers have concentrated on the benefits of dialogue journals for students, but the process offers equal benefits to teachers as well:

> I am struck continually by the isolation, the loneliness of teaching. . . . The dialogue journal is one way to alter this isolation, and as such, it represents one essential human truth: we become and remain human not through the acquisition of factual knowledge or skills but through participation in social communities which respond to us as persons. (Staton 1987, 60)

I believed that dialogue journal writing could provide one way in which we might develop a responsive community. Further, the connections between dialogue journal writing and emancipatory constructs of teacher-as-researcher appeared strong: both approaches place high value on shared searches for and constructions of knowledge, and both view knowledge as provisional and open to question.

I thought that this written form of dialogue among us could enhance our attempts to understand and to create interactive and consensual forms of inquiry. Still, the dialogue journal represents one of several points within our interactions that places me in the role as teacher-leader, and I here again want to acknowledge a particular direction and form that I suggested as part of our research context; this suggestion contributed to the boundaries as well as possible expansions in our explorations of the teacher-as-researcher construct. Yet it ultimately provided both context and process for us to consider, in deeper ways than anticipated, the nature of voice, dialogue, and writing as problematic aspects of an emancipatory discourse.

I did suggest that we might read and respond to one another's journals so as to remove myself as sole responder; the others did not wish to do so, and that pattern remained fairly constant well into our second year of work together. At that point, members of the group expressed interest in writing to one another as well as to me. However, group members' initial reasons for not collectively sharing their writing included lack of time and uncertainty about the process itself, since none of these teachers had kept a journal with any regularity or particular focus. Further, when I offered to share the first journal entry of the one teacher, Cheryl, whose initial inquiry early that summer had prompted my conceptualization of a research group, the others did not want to read her writing or my response. Each expressed a need to begin as he or she felt ready and as a research focus began to emerge.

Although they initially rejected a formalized sharing and responding to one another's journal writing, nevertheless individuals have revealed in our collective meetings both the content and process of their writing and of our dialogues. Our writing functions differently for each of us, and we have traced those changing functions throughout our work together. We did begin, however, with an assumption that the journal writing would provide one form of dialogue, albeit partial, among us.

In addition to the regular meetings, and the reflective and dialogical journal writing, we tape-record each of our sessions; those

27

recordings provide yet another context for our studies, in that they allow us to return to our questions as well as to see movement in our explorations.

Separate Spaces: Individual Assumptions and Expectations

Each of the five teachers had been a student in one or more of my graduate classes, and thus was familiar not only with my general approaches to teaching and to curriculum inquiry but also with the backgrounds and viewpoints of the other members of our research group. They recognized that my overt assumptions about appropriate modes of research for educational contexts were represented in the courses I taught on qualitative approaches; they knew my commitment to revealing the value-laden nature of curriculum in a variety of personal and social contexts, evident in the form and content of my curriculum courses.

In turn, I recognized that these approaches often created discomfort among my students because of their contrast to the predominantly behaviorist and experimentally oriented nature of most theoretical and research approaches in our graduate programs. However, because we were meeting without the formal structures and confinements of a course, these teachers were able to reveal their interest in and their hesitations about the nature, form, and purpose of our explorations of alternative conceptions of research, teaching, and curriculum. I too was able to reveal the uncertain, and, at best, meandering directions that had pointed me to this attempted collaborative investigation. Meeting on our own time, with no course credit and evaluative component to frame our pursuits, we agreed that we met freely, motivated by curiosity and a sense of possible connections to one another and to our work as educators.

The following are initial descriptions of each participant and her or his educational setting. These descriptions are drawn largely from transcriptions of our first meetings and excerpts from our dialogue journal writings that address some underlying assumptions and frame each person's preliminary focus in our studies. Embedded in these descriptions is our initial belief in the necessity of a research stance that, as Clandinin (1986) argues, credits teachers' knowledge and that views teachers as people whose personal as well as professional lives constitute, reveal, and frame their thought. As the collaboration

28

continued and developed, subsequent tracings of our work pointed to more specific attempts to extend this stance. We began and continue to examine the assumption that the research process can enable people to change by encouraging self-reflection and a deeper understanding of their particular situations (Lather 1986).

The School Psychologist

As we began our collaboration, Kevin had worked for five years as a child psychologist in an elementary school; he was just beginning to work also in his district's high school three days a week. At our first meeting, he noted that he was having to adjust his approach to the students: "It's a big shift from hearing about Saturday morning cartoons to dealing with sex and drugs." He also felt shifts in his perceptions of his role as psychologist and in his relationships with other professionals in this new setting (from our September 20, 1986, meeting):

> I'm not sure yet where I stand at the high school. I'm used to the routine and the comfort level and the more intimate feeling of an elementary school. And yet I'm not a behaviorist, and that's what most elementary school psychologists do—set up behavior-mod programs. So, with a lot of what I do, I never have felt like I totally fit in.

Much of Kevin's work with the elementary school children, especially, requires testing and application of behaviorist techniques to "improve" the children's behavior in the classroom. Kevin voiced his uncomfortable feelings with the limitations of these approaches, and spoke of his own counseling as centered on establishing a relationship with his student clients and, over time, developing an understanding of the person behind the test scores. At our first meeting, Kevin spoke briefly about his seminary study and background in philosophical inquiry as influences on his interest in the reflective component of both his professional role and our collaborative project.

As he spoke of his background and especially of the ways in which he never quite fit in with the test-score mentality of the elementary school structure, other members in our group expressed some surprise and relief at Kevin's remarks. We all were surprised that Kevin would feel at all uncomfortable anywhere he worked, for we perceived him to be easy-going, affable, and gentle and sensitive in his relations with others. At the same time, we were able to laugh, a little bit at least, at this assumption that contradicted what each of us often felt in our own situations, even when we appeared to be "just fine."

Our tentative laughter reminded us of how often we summarize others' situations, and base our assessments on assumptions of congruence between countenance and feelings. The laughter also broke the tension of our first session, and we then also could express various degrees of relief in Kevin's verbalizing feelings that we all shared to some degree in our individual contexts.

Cheryl noted her difficulties with having to keep such "tight records" about the learning-disabled children with whom she worked, and Katherine spoke briefly about how relieved she was to hear that someone else had trouble with what she saw as more and more rigid approaches to elementary teaching and curriculum. Beth spoke of her constant feeling of pressure to "have all the answers." Marjorie spoke of her struggle to figure out "where she belonged," and I noted my feelings of displacement within the structured doctoral program.

In one brief discussion, Kevin had opened up some areas and issues with which we all felt some discomfort in our individual educational settings and experiences. Issues of curriculum, teaching, and personal expectations for ourselves as educators emerged quickly. Without any intention to do so and without naming the connections to our larger contexts, Kevin had set our explorations into motion.

In our first meeting, Kevin also expressed an interest in the journal writing possibilities of our work. He regularly wrote accounts of his sessions with students, following the typical clinical case study approach utilized by most school psychologists. He spoke of a possible variation on this process:

> At the high school, it seems like it might be easier than I'm thinking right now, because the kids are trying to make their way on their own, and in a way, I can see how they are just like kindergarteners, trying to move away from home, only on a bigger scale. So, in my work with them, because I'm not going to be so pressured to do the behavior-mod kind of thing, I think I can focus more on them. I was thinking, as we were talking about journal writing, that maybe I could have my high school clients keep journals and that would really help me to respond to them, even in writing.

Kevin thus saw his work with his high school students as his focus in our teacher/researcher construct, and initially, his journal writing contained descriptive accounts of his students and their problems and situational contexts. These accounts resembled, in tone as well as content, the typical case study reporting that he had been doing for years. Kevin noted the difficulties that he was having in doing his own journal writing in addition to his case-load reporting and in differentiating the purpose of each (from our October 7, 1986, meeting):

> When I started writing for this, first I found that I had a hard time getting started, just getting myself to do it. I was afraid that it was going to be a chore, because writing isn't usually easy for me. Then I found that I didn't have enough time; once I would get started, I found that I was writing on all different levels or maybe thinking on all different levels.
>
> And I write differently on the days that I'm in the high school than when I'm in the elementary school. In the high school I'm a counselor and I see about fifteen kids. Some days I would write about one or two kids, but I could really focus on them. But in the elementary school, I feel as much an administrator as a psychologist, because I'm talking to the teachers all the time about the kids and I have all kinds of paper work, and I really feel pulled apart. And so the things I write about there are more about how I feel pulled apart. And I'm also getting a better view of how involved and complex the counseling relationship is as I write about it all. The other thing that is bothering me, though, is that when I'm in the high school, I can really write about those kids, I can really concentrate on them. I find it easy to enter into their world.
>
> But I guard this journal with my life because I'm not sure sometimes that I should put all of this down and so I can feel a shift in my writing already to me and my feelings rather than my analysis of my cases.

Although Kevin felt "pulled apart" in his elementary setting, then, that context provided him with a reason for slowly changing the content and tone of his journal entries. His fragmented feelings also prompted him to begin not only to reflect upon those feelings but also to consider the structures within that elementary school which contributed to his sense of never quite fitting in. Furthermore, his discomfort in writing about high school clients and his difficulties in asking them to keep journals signaled his uncertainty about appropriate forums for our dialogue journal writing. His decision to focus more upon his own role within counseling sessions reflects these dilemmas. At the same time, Kevin's decision also points to the functional and self-generated nature of the journal writing itself.

Kevin's attempts to grapple in writing with his "pulled-apart" feeling and to differentiate between his case-load writing and our journal writing thus called attention to the difficulties as well as benefits of writing in our explorations. As one of the group members who initially was skeptical of his own writing ability and of his willingness to devote the time and concentration to journal writing, Kevin now continues to utilize a great deal of journal writing. He exemplifies throughout our narratives the ways in which writing is a support for him in our explorations as well as in his daily work.

In the first few months of our collaboration, Kevin started to focus more on his own reactions and perceptions in his counseling sessions, especially in the elementary school, rather than on his clients in the high school on whom he initially thought it might be easier to do "research." As he also began to look at the structures that seemed to reinforce his fragmented feelings, he began to raise questions about his understandings of himself as psychologist, and about the interplay of the contexts within which he worked. I responded to some of his initial inquiries (from my October 13, 1986, response):

> You've started to talk a lot about your sense of fragmentation and your concerns about not being totally present as you work through the routine testing of the kids, in particular. Some of that fragmentation must have to do with being in so many different physical places during the course of a school week, yes? I would have a hard time figuring out where I was when—is this part of the issue for you? I've noticed that you are starting to use a lot of physical metaphors in your writing—feeling "pulled apart" and not "fitting in." Do you have to segment your thinking every day into high school and elementary students so as to keep clear about what it is that you have to do in each place? Seems like you have to make huge mental leaps between the two—is this part of the fragmentation too?

As we wrote back and forth about this initial theme of fragmentation, Kevin began to elaborate upon the physical metaphors which he used to describe his feelings as he attempted to juggle his work within two disparate contexts. For example, he began to notice his discomfort with some of his physically disabled students in the BOCES classroom (from an October 17, 1986, journal entry):[1]

> Whenever I go to a BOCES special ed. school, I reflect on my reasons for choosing psychology which initially were to work with more disturbed children than I see now in the public schools I work in. The children in the

BOCES I was visiting are very obviously physically, emotionally and/or mentally handicapped. I wonder how comfortable and effective I would be working with these children.

In a November 4th, 1986, entry, Kevin is more specific about his feelings:

I'm testing a third-grade girl who is a transfer into school from the city. She has spina bifada. . . . I could feel myself tightening up when I first met her. I still have a problem initially meeting a physically disabled child—I stumble on the disability at first—although working with Danny and with Mike at the high school, the orthopedically handicapped students, has helped me work through some of my feelings.

Part of my response to that journal entry included more questions:

What is amazing to me as I read through your journal is the number of kids that you see in one week and the extent of their problems! And then you wonder if you would be effective with the more disabled kids whom you see in the BOCES setting, and I'm thinking to myself that I would be overwhelmed by the kids' problems that you deal with in your "regular" settings. Do you ever go home depressed or feeling that you just can't ever listen to one more problem? Or, I guess a deeper question is, do you feel powerless in the face of their individual contexts and problems over which you have very little control?

Kevin started to look at the ways in which his physical metaphors pointed to the confinement and disjuncture that he often felt within the schooling spaces where he did his counseling work. He responded to the question of feeling powerless by noting the "tightening-up" that he felt, not only with his physically disabled students but also with his surroundings and the implied expectations that he felt others had for his work. He spoke of feeling "on the spot" when another more experienced high school counselor offered to talk with him every week about his cases, even though he appreciated her support and insightful comments. Kevin also wrote about feeling "in the middle," as he often was called upon to negotiate or decide issues that arose among his fellow psychologists as well as among the elementary classroom teachers.

As we moved through the introductory segments of our work together, Kevin's interest in his journal writing as a place to reflect on the contexts in which he worked as a school psychologist continued to grow. He began speaking in our group meetings about the physical metaphors that filled his writing, and started to talk about the ways in which he wanted to look at some of the standard structures and expectations of schooling as possibly influencing his sense of "tightness." He knew his own expectations for himself influenced some of those feelings; he now began to talk about our researching processes as providing the challenge for him to look beyond himself and to the converging influences of culture and society, including parental, collegial, and administrative expectations, upon his conceptions of himself as a school psychologist. As Kevin noted in our December 1, 1986, meeting:

> I'm starting to get comfortable with our research group. Before we started this, I felt like I was making some connections between my work and the issues that we talked about in class, like all the various forms of hidden curriculum that influence what we expect from students and teachers and ourselves. But then I would go to work, and I would lose the connections, especially if I felt myself "tightening up" over some kid or difficult situation. This is helping me to keep the connections in my head, at least, or now in my writing. I think this is helping me to see further and bigger.

We all laughed at this last comment, but in wanting to "see further and bigger," Kevin had captured a bit of what we all were beginning to think it might take to become challengers in our educational worlds.

The First-Grade Teacher

As we began our study, Katherine had been teaching elementary children for almost a decade, and she was nearing the completion of her course work for her Professional Diploma, a program that required thirty graduate hours beyond a Master's degree.

Katherine is caring, enthusiastic, and very positive in her work with her first-graders, yet worries about the individual problems and difficult home situations that characterize many of her children's lives. She had agreed with Kevin's descriptions of feeling "pulled apart" within the elementary school; yet Katherine chose in our preliminary meetings to focus on one child in her classroom, Valerie, rather than on her voiced sense of frustration within her school setting.

Valerie, a shy child, often hid her face behind her arm when talking to Katherine, and made remarks about her mother's displeasure with her. Katherine was concerned about Valerie's worrying that her mother would hit her or that her mother thought she was "stupid." In our first meeting on September 20, 1986, Katherine told us of Valerie's quiet yet revealing remarks, and then said firmly, "I like this little girl. I think she's worth it. I refuse to let this little girl go by."

Thus, Katherine was able to quickly declare her wish to focus on Valerie, not in overt ways in the classroom that would detract from her attention to the other children, but in her writing and reflection within our group context. An early journal entry reveals Katherine's concern with the effects of this covert attention (from a September 26, 1986, journal entry):

Can my special attention be feeding into how she behaves? It's not that I reduce my expectations or demands for her. Yet I find myself often very surprised and excited when she volunteers and gets an answer correct. I believe that Valerie can learn. She is not a slow child. She has many strengths and I hope through encouragement, she'll be ok.

By October, Katherine was becoming aware of the complexity of Valerie's home situation. She spoke several times in our meetings of the difficulties that teachers face when confronted with children's problems that originate outside the classroom, and she also spoke of the ethical dimensions of teachers' boundaries and possible courses of action. As Katherine began to reveal her frustrations and confusions with the boundaries of her role as teacher, her journal writing as well as her dialogue within our group began to focus on her own expectations for herself (from an October 1, 1986, journal entry):

What I've been thinking about is where my role as teacher ends and where parents take over. With Valerie I feel that I'm trying to "undo" what her parents do at home. For example, "My mommy says my work is ugly," or "My mommy says there is something wrong with me." How much can I really do to help with this situation? I want to suggest to Valerie's mother, Mrs. T., that Valerie be tested so that she could get some extra help, emotional as well as academic. My principal says that this will never work. Mrs. T. is a famous difficult person around here.

35

As Katherine pursued possible avenues of outside help for Valerie, her journal writing reflected her frustration with both the parental and administrative limitations that she felt were being imposed upon her role as teacher. I noted these difficulties in my first journal response to her:

> There's so much struggle happening on all different levels with Valerie, yes? You write about feeling the pull of wanting to be respected for your professional expertise and knowledge and yet wanting to acknowledge the roles of parents in the education of their children. And so you talk, like Kevin does, of feeling pulled apart by these conflicting desires. Do you think that being an early childhood educator always involves this kind of conflict? That is, so much of your work with children has to do with nurturing and providing experiences that allow children to grow and develop in all ways. So I can see how you would feel angry with Mrs. T. because she seems to be messing up her end of the deal. How could she say those things to Valerie? Of course, the other question is, does she say those things to Valerie? You ask these questions throughout your writing thus far. Does Valerie's brother say these same things? Can you ask the counselor and your principal about this, as the mother is now coming in for conferences about the brother's troubles in school too?

As Katherine kept raising questions in our sessions and in our dialogue journal writing, she began to shift her focus from Valerie to her own grapplings with conflicting demands and emotions that she felt were limiting and sometimes even distorting the nature of her work as a first-grade teacher. She expressed these feelings in a series of journal entries as well as in an early November meeting of our group (from an October 15, 1986, journal entry):

> My feelings regarding my own expectations for Valerie—I feel they have changed to some degree. I think I was almost "afraid of" Valerie in that I did not want to upset her. I found myself accepting work from her that was usually (for any other child) not acceptable. So I have to be careful to not impose my own limitations on her. I really do think that she can learn, so I need to treat her that way.
>
>   I would like to think that her parents and my principal have enough faith in my judgement to accept my suggestion to explore other possibilities (through testing, counseling) for Valerie. I would like to think that I am capable of explaining fully, yet tenderly, why I feel it would be in Valerie's best interest. . . . This all brings me back to an earlier question—How far does a teacher go? Does my role end somewhere and in that somewhere, do I lose my ability for input, for effect on a child? Are there boundaries within

which teachers must function? There probably are, morally, of course. But do I get to have a say in figuring out where they are? Was my principal reminding me of my boundaries as teacher today? Is that why I felt put off by him when I asked about counseling for Valerie again? Or did I feel he had overstepped his boundaries and was now interferring in my role as classroom teacher? I don't know. It's hard to figure out all the "shoulds" that rule my responses in that school.

With these self-generated questions, Katherine opened up new areas of reflection on her role and her expectations for herself within the boundaries that she had constructed, as well as those that had been constructed for her as teacher. As she began to push against these boundaries, to question the reasons for the limits that she felt were defining her role, Katherine began to look at herself as teacher in some new and, for her, some startling ways. Her research focus became herself, and, as she began to pose questions about her role and function within the classroom, Katherine withdrew somewhat from the journal writing. She spoke in our initial sessions of her difficulties with writing and with "finding time, a place in her life" to do the writing. At our November 11, 1986, meeting, Katherine again spoke of her feelings about writing:

I just can't seem to get it all down. My mind just keeps going, and the questions just keep coming.

One of her last journal entries for quite a while hinted at the sometimes painful and frightening aspects of her questioning (from a November 2, 1986, entry):

The little ones demand so much of my attention. They want to share everything. Sometimes, I just can't take another sharing session; I've seen all the Transformers and Cabbage Patch dolls I can stand. I know that sometimes I have no patience, and I'll quickly comment about a child's toy or sharing object. I just can't muster up enough enthusiasm every time. I've noticed too that when I'm tired or upset about something, I can be sarcastic with some children. . . . My sarcasm is usually the last straw. It comes out when I have nothing left in me to give. . . . And that's when I feel overwhelmed. I feel limited. But it's what to do with these feelings that I want to address. Acknowledging is one thing. Doing something is another. But is it within my power to control/or to do something about? . . . The dimensions of teaching are so vast—I guess that's why I feel limited or overwhelmed.

I wrote back to Katherine in a November 4, 1986, entry:

> You do seem to be questioning quite a bit your understandings of your own expectations for yourself. You mention your worry about your tired and therefore sarcastic responses to the children, and you've mentioned quite a few times feeling limited as a teacher. What I wonder about is if these issues seem new to you? Is this the first year that you have been concerned/aware of the effects of routine and repetition upon your teaching? Is it that your class this year seems to harbor such distinct differences and levels?
>
> Is Valerie symbolic for you in your interest yet frustration with her situation? In other words, do many of your accumulated anxieties and questions seem to come into focus through her? And is this the strongest that you have felt about these conflicts and ambiguities? Guess that I'm exploring with you some possible questions and frustrations that have surfaced, especially through the story of Valerie. And I could be asking all the wrong questions here, but compared to some of your responses and statements in our graduate class sessions, these seem like new, or at least recently surfaced, feelings for you. Where am I on this? Write back, or don't—you know that you don't have to. Is the writing contributing to these feelings? Or is this just a place where you've been able to express them?

My own uncertainties and fears of imposing the journal writing on the group members surfaced here, but Katherine, in our group meeting of November 11, 1986, picked up on the questions about which we had been writing rather than on the issue of the journal writing, per se:

> I keep thinking about your questions, and about why I originally picked Valerie as my research focus. I think that I have a real need to prove myself as a teacher, as a professional. It goes back somewhat to when I finally got into the primary grades, where I really wanted to be, and then the principal told me that I had to follow some time management charts that another teacher had created. This teacher shared her ideas grudgingly with me; I resented not being able to do what I thought was appropriate for my kids, and yet I spent two years thinking that this was what I had to do. I felt like such an appendage. So now, that teacher is gone, and I think that I have to prove to the principal that I can do something on my own.
>
> And yet, with Valerie, I've picked an almost impossible situation to say I'm going to do something about this. And when Valerie's mother finally agreed last week to have Valerie tested, I thought, aha!, I did it. But it's such a small step, and nothing is finished.
>
> In some ways, I feel like I'm trying to leap up, not just to get the principal's approval, but to have some feelings of making a difference with the kids and of having some true sharing among some teachers, not just the

competitive stuff that the time management charts created among us. I guess that Valerie's situation has allowed me to look at myself in relation to all these other things going on in my school.

At this meeting, Katherine talked at length about the pain that she felt as she began to unravel the various threads that tangled her responses to her principal, the other teachers with whom she worked, and her students. Her question, "What can I do?", posed earlier in her journal entries and now in our group meetings, pointed to her feelings of limitation and isolation as a teacher and to her uncertainties about the possibilities of resisting or changing the competitive and individualistic situation in her school. Her question has become a major point within our investigations, for we can think of no better way to challenge our limiting situations as well as the possibilities for emancipatory teaching and research than to constantly ask, "What can we do?"

Like Kevin, Katherine opened areas for our collective investigations, and provided another vantage point from which to view and pursue our work. In our December 1, 1986, meeting, Katherine declared:

> I can see that my focus in this work has changed. But I can also see how my understandings of this work itself are changing. I thought, when we began, that my research focus had to be something out there. Now I think my project is me.

Katherine then expressed a desire to continue her unraveling of the threads of others' expectations that surrounded her expectations for herself as teacher. She noted in this meeting that she still expected herself always to be able to give to the children, both emotionally and academically, and she had to fight feelings of deficiency if her emotions or physical tiredness intruded upon that "giving" expectation. She also raised the issue of wanting to be seen as a competent professional in her principal's eyes, and she connected this, for the first time in our discussions, to our graduate classroom analyses of elementary teaching as "women's work." Katherine, in this meeting, expressed a desire to look at her own teaching situation as one in which she could begin to see the contradictions between conceptions of "competent professional" and "women's work."

To these connections that Katherine made we responded with excited support and with analogous descriptions of the limitations of our often hierarchical teaching situations. Kevin noted that Katherine's desire to "leap up," to be seen as a person within the bureaucracy, reminded him of why he often felt himself "tightening" and unable to "leap up," as it were.

As we began to make these collective as well as individual connections, Katherine withdrew temporarily from our dialogue journal writing. She began to feel most comfortable within the context of our group meetings and this was where she continued to share her understandings and constantly emerging questions. She spoke about her uneasiness with the journal writing in our meeting of February 2, 1987:

> I do have a fear of writing. It's so permanent, and I know that someone will read it. I'm afraid that maybe I'll learn too much if I write it all down, and I'm not ready for it all at once. Actually, I surprised myself when I said I would be a part of this group. I wasn't really involved in high school or college. I really didn't share with people or get that involved with groups. So I was really surprised at how much I wanted to be part of this look at teacher-as-researcher. But I had to find out, had to be able to share here first with you all. I had to find out how much I could share, and the writing seemed to make it come too quickly. I had to know that I could talk first, that I could really participate first. Then maybe I can write some more.

Katherine's willingness to reveal her fears and resistance to the journal writing indicated to all of us, and most importantly, to herself, that, in fact, she was able to share her own feelings and ideas. At the same time, she was not willing to replicate others' approaches in order to participate in the group, and, given her own articulated struggle with the "shoulds" of life, she saw that fact as important in acknowledging her ability to make her own sense of things.

Further, Katherine's resistance to the journal writing points to a variety of ways in which one may participate and construct one's own emancipatory version of teacher-as-researcher. For Katherine, the dialogue that ensued among the group members served as a framework within which she could examine her own as well as others' notions of teaching and research. She noted that the response from us began to function as a key that unlocked her own response, rather than as a cue telling her how to respond (from our December 1, 1986, meeting):

40

I think that I am beginning to listen for myself first, rather than for what others say first. And so I'm not so locked into what I "should" say in return, like to the principal so that he will think I'm a good teacher. This is new. I'm beginning to hear myself, and I do not want to speak with someone else's voice!

The Department Chairperson

When Beth responded to my invitation to join in these explorations, she was serving as a mathematics department chairperson of a junior high school in a district where she had taught for eighteen years. In addition to her administrative duties, she taught several math classes.

During the month between our picnic lunch and our first scheduled meeting, Beth had started to keep a journal. We had spoken of journal-writing possibilities at that picnic, although we only formalized our willingness to attempt dialogue journal writing at our first meeting in September. As we forged the plans for our journal-writing procedures, and as some of the group members started to wonder out loud about what they could begin to look at in terms of becoming researching teachers, Beth finally spoke about the journal she had already begun. She talked excitedly about the ways in which her journal writing helped to "put her back in touch with the kids":

> One of the things that has bothered me in the last three years is the job I have. As chair of the department these last three years, I have pulled away from the classroom. And I love thinking about the classroom and kids' reactions and things that go on there. Now, that's just secondary, and I'm not sure about my own personal directions because of these shifts. Do I want to stay in the classroom or do I want to move on into more administrative work? Or is it possible to take the time to focus on the classroom, really focus like I used to, and still do this other job? This journal writing that I've done so far has really brought me back into the classroom and my focus on kids and what happens to me too in there.

At our first meeting, Beth talked about the possibility of having her seventh-grade math class keep journals about their problems and thoughts while learning math. She was looking for a way, even in this first organization meeting, in which she could replicate some of our group research processes. As we discussed the possible processes of our dialogue journal writing, Beth said that she would like to engage

41

in dialogue journal writing with her seventh-graders as a way to continue her renewed sense of connection to the classroom. I encouraged her to try this, and spoke about her idea as one example of the kinds of activities that writing process researchers were encouraging within the concept of "writing across the curriculum." As I noted examples of journal writing within various subject areas as representative of many teachers' awareness of writing as one way of "knowing," Beth interrupted me:

> I'm excited that kids might find the journal writing helpful in learning about math. But what I want to know is, can these things that we are attempting in our classes and here together create change? I think that the self-esteem of teachers is low, and I want to find ways for us to feel better about what we do. But do you think that others will look at all this, and want to package it and take it on the road? I'm so afraid of the possible distortions of what we're trying to do.

We laughed at the marketing possibilities of "emancipatory pedagogy and research kits" and yet we all had experienced the packaged nature of many educational innovation and in-service programs. We shared a strong uneasiness about "deficit" models of staff and curriculum development that implicitly assumed deficiencies within teachers and that presented prescriptive remedies and packaged answers to alleviate those deficiencies. In fact, our concerns about teachers' low self-esteem as embedded within these deficit models had, in part, prompted our initial connections to one another and to our search for emancipatory forms of teaching and research.

Beth shared a recent experience with yet another deficit model of staff development, and admitted that her anxiety about "packaging" was reinforced by this encounter:

> My principal had gone to a workshop on writing for administrators. And in our first administrators' meeting this year, you could see that she was excited about this. And so she started to lay out her goals for the year, and she said that she wanted us all to keep journals. And I had two feelings about this: on the one hand, I wanted to be the one who introduced this idea in our administrators' group, because I'm so excited about what we are doing here. I admit it, I wanted to be the one. [We laugh, appreciating Beth's honesty.] On the other hand, I thought to myself, "you're going too fast, you can't make people do this." I could feel myself bubbling over this as she just continued on, telling us how and when we would do the journal writing. And

I just didn't want her to ruin this because the journal writing had already become so special to me. And that's the kind of thing that destroys the quality and possibilities—telling people that they have to do something without letting them the discover the possibilities in it for themselves. So now I have a fear about what we're doing and I want to say, "please don't destroy what we have." I guess that this is just the ongoing battle—you just have to put your point of view out there and then let people decide for themselves.

Beth initially continued her research focus on the problems and benefits of dialogue journal writing with her seventh-graders. In an October 1, 1986, journal entry, she noted her positive feelings about the process:

I've written back to all of the students and have found that it's a great way to offer suggestions individually. In the past, it would have been a blanket statement and I would just hope they would pick up whatever message I gave.

However, as excited as she was about her writing with the seventh-graders, Beth's attentions were directed quickly into her own journal writing as a place for reflection and for sorting out conflicting pressures in her work. She began to identify as dichotomous her feelings of having to "have the right answers" and yet wanting to have the "time and support for these reflective processes that we share" before she could "even begin to think about answers." She began to feel these pressures mount as, early in the fall of our first year of meetings, she was asked to apply for the position of Evaluator within her school district. Beth brought her concerns about this possible job change to our October 7, 1986, meeting:

You know, our work together already has such an impact on me in terms of pulling me from all the crazy hectic frenzy of school and helping me to look at myself and at that school too. What I see is that this is so important that I may change because of it. But I don't want to make rules for others to change. Is that what an evaluator would do?

Marjorie responded:

I just think that what we are trying to do here, trying to look at things from different points of view, is what you could do as an evaluator too. There's no one who is in a better position right now in schools to effect change than an

43

evaluator. You could really encourage people to look at curriculum and teaching and research from different perspectives.

In her reply, Beth again pointed to the dichotomies that our work together was highlighting:

> What I have to determine is if that's what my school district administrators would want me to do in this position. I have a feeling that the encouraging of multiple perspectives isn't what they have in mind for this job!

As she wrestled with her decision about whether or not to even apply for this evaluator's position, Beth felt the shift in her journal writing. She noted that she still felt more connected to her students than she had in quite a while, but that she needed the journal writing for herself as a place in which she could struggle with the dilemmas that this potential job change posed for her (from a journal entry of October 16, 1986):

> I just don't experience anywhere else in my job as teacher/department chair the level of thinking that I experience in our group and in my journal. I realize that I'm starting to struggle to get back to that level of thinking in my daily school life, and I can't quite get there. Could this job as evaluator be a place where I could do that? What I deal with every day now just feels so far away from that level of thinking. I just want to have that more on a full-time professional and personal basis. And my journal is allowing me to keep in touch with my dissatisfactions and my just as strong fears about changing jobs. Am I searching for too much?

As she continued to debate her possible job change, Beth began to use her journal to record her personal conflicts and apprehensions about taking the position as district evaluator, and, at the same time, to note the places in her work environment where she felt less or more tension. In a November 10, 1986, journal entry, she writes of her growing confusion:

> I keep thinking about where I fit in. How could I have worked in one school district for so long and still feel sometimes like I don't fit in? Right now, it feels tougher to fit into the classroom and feel good about it. This time, I wrote [a list] of why I want the job and why I don't. The whys outdid the nots, 9–2. . . . I can't focus on my job now or the kids; it's difficult. I can't even think about questions to ask.

Unlike Kevin, who continued to write about his students even as he also began to wrestle with his "pulled apart" feelings and to examine the sources of those fragmented feelings, Beth essentially dropped her research focus on her seventh-grade students, and made her dichotomous feelings the focus of her research. And unlike Katherine, who was struggling with similar feelings of displacement but who articulated her research focus in our group meetings rather than in journal writing, Beth began to write continually.

Her journal began to function as a sounding space within which Beth wrestled with the issues surrounding her ambivalence toward remaining a classroom teacher or becoming a full-time administrator. Beth, in essence, created her own dialogue journal; even though she and I continue to exchange frequent and lengthy journal dialogues with each other, in many respects Beth's responses to herself are the more illuminating of the exchanges. Typically, Beth chronicles external events, then, often in list form, narrows her attention to the emotional responses to those events. Finally, she writes of her analysis, as far as she says she is able to see, of the dynamics of her reactions and feelings (from a January 20, 1987, journal entry):

> Here I tend to look at things like I do in class. I attempt to focus in on commonalities and look to see how I have changed. I look to question, to pull apart, to attack with hopes for a clearer understanding. Now, here's the weird part . . . as I am writing, I realize that that's the way I operate. Examine, put aside, examine, pick a little, reflect, put aside and finally . . . go for it.

Beth's journal writing exemplifies the particular role of self-response as an "inner intermediating process" (Heath 1987) that potentially enables a writer to hear and to trust what Freedman (1985) calls the "inner voice." At the same time, Beth's willingness to ask questions, both of herself and of us, points to the necessity of "internal" as well as "external" response in creating "spaces where dialogue can take place."

By asking, "Is there a right way to do this?" and by attempting to immediately connect our explorations to her educational setting, Beth pointed to a major theme and its embedded contradictions with which we continue to grapple in our work together. She is insistent in her search for processes and approaches in our collaborative work that might extend beyond our group and have potential use in the

45

daily lives of teachers and students. Yet she recognizes the press within her educator roles as teacher and administrator to "always have the answers" and to point to the "right" ways in which to do teaching and administrative work. The tensions between the evolving processes of our collaboration and the prescriptive mandates within which she attempts those processes remain a major conflict within Beth's educational life. In her discussion of these tensions, she continues her role within our group as our insistent questioner.

In that role, which she established in our very first meeting, she presses us to articulate connections between our collective explorations and the possible ways in which other educators might engage in similar self-reflexive research. She also constantly draws attention to the difficulties of enacting such possibilities by sharing her sense of dichotomies. As she continues to highlight the ironies that she has identified among her desires to create change and yet to "let people decide for themselves", to have the right answers and yet to avoid the prescription and packaging of those answers for herself or for others, Beth struggles. With the rest of us, she works not only to search for evidence "of the forces that have diminished us" but also to "recover our own possibilities" as a way of narrowing the dichotomies between our public and private worlds.

The Special Educator

For several years, I had been thinking about the emancipatory possibilities of teacher-as-researcher as I worked on writing in-service programs with classroom teachers. However, it was Cheryl's curiosity about learning disabled students' abilities to think critically and metaphorically that led to my actual invitation to her and the others.

Cheryl and I had spoken throughout the previous year about possible dissertation topics emerging from her special education teaching interests and responsibilities. When I suggested that she start to record her hunches and observations about the learning disabled (LD) students with whom she was working, Cheryl's excitement about her journal writing encouraged me to approach her about dialogue journal writing between the two of us as she continued her investigations. Our journal exchanges during the early part of the summer of 1986, and our excitement about our joint research processes, created a connection between us that I wanted to extend to others in the form of an exploratory research group. Thus, Cheryl's willingness to engage in our tentative attempts at self-reflexive research approaches provided crucial encouragement to me to take action on the issues with which I had been grappling for quite a while. The invitation that I issued at that picnic lunch was a first form of action.

As we began our collaborative work, Cheryl continued to focus upon the ten learning disabled children, ages eleven to fourteen, with whom she had been working. She was interested in exploring the differences between learning disabled and "normal" students' abilities to integrate, respond to, and evaluate information. She chose music as the subject area within which to investigate these processes because children could listen and respond to music in emotional as well as in more linear, "school-like" ways. Cheryl thought that her research focus would continue to be upon ways in which to expand the range of LD students' task approach skills and cognitive strategies, reflecting the nature and orientation of much of the research in special education. She began to write about her work with these children and with her fellow teachers, who also were working closely with these children in small resource-room groups, and who agreed to participate in her pilot research. However, as she continued her research, which included tape-recordings of the music sessions and interviews with the students and teachers, she became intrigued with the responses not only of the students but also of the teachers (from a July 9, 1986, entry in Cheryl's journal):

> Some of the discussion about the song that we played for the kids, and the LD kids' answers really showed interesting thought. What it seemed from listening to the second week's tapes was that the kids' answers depend on the teacher and his/her rapport with the child. By "it" I mean the quality and quantity of the answers depended, to some extent, on the willingness of the child to work with the teacher. Also, I noticed that not enough time was given to the students to answer question #4—the comparison question. And when I did the questions myself, I saw I needed much time to mull #4 over and come up with an answer I considered suitable. If I wanted time, I want to make sure the students have more time for that question too.

Cheryl wrote daily in her journal as she conducted her research, and she quickly began to note that her areas of discomfort centered not on students' abilities to respond to the music but rather on the teachers' inabilities to respond to deviant or atypical responses from the children (from a July 16, 1986, entry in Cheryl's journal):

> I feel I should tell the teachers not only about what I did—to give kids more "wait" time to think about question #4—but to let them compare it with anything, not just a song. The thought is there, but not only a musical answer is required—any comparison is good. It seems more and more to me that some teachers are very able to probe, establish a relationship with the kids and thus get responses from them, even though the LD kids clearly have no experience with this kind of thinking. Other teachers ask flatly and don't probe gently and so get flat answers.

Cheryl's concern with the "flat" nature of some of the LD teachers' interactions with their students framed the emerging direction of her research focus within our group. By the end of the summer, just as our group was coalescing, Cheryl was seeing her research from a new angle. She expressed concern about the typical drills that some of the teachers depended upon in working with these children, and she started to consider the ways in which teaching approaches, including her own, could limit and thus determine, to some extent, students' possible responses (from a July 22, 1986, entry):

> Once again, the LD kids seem to need us to pull out the comparisons, not volunteering responses unless they are helped with leading questions, while the non-LD kids volunteer to answer why they chose certain answers. It seems the non-LD kids have had much more positive experiences and more experience with thinking about a question or idea and then coming up with an answer. . . . The LD kids are often taught in drill, teacher-directed ways. It does not seem that the ones who are participating in this study have had much chance to use their minds and to think. That is a problem which arises from the fact that they have so much to catch up on, in basic skills, that their teachers probably do not slot time for more creative pursuits. But they need time to think and to write. They need opportunities to express their opinions and to think before they answer quickly.

By Cheryl's September 5, 1986, journal entry, she was directing her attention to the nature of teachers' responses within the context of her pilot study:

> When thinking about the teachers in my pilot, I think that the good ones were the flexible ones. If they were open to accepting different answers from

students, trying to build on what students say, helping them to go further, expanding upon their thoughts, then students would be encouraged to at least try. Some of the teachers who were not as effective, in my estimation, were more rigid and thought along one "track," so to speak. They had a preconceived notion of what the answer should be, and if a student went off in a different direction, they'd say, "No. But what about . . . ." They were clearly putting their ideas of the answer as the way students should think and respond.

In our group's initial meetings, Cheryl talked a bit about her preliminary attempts at becoming a researching teacher, and noted that her perceptions of research were starting to change, as a result of the journal writing and our exchanges. She noted that her original research conceptions were themselves "flat" in that they did not take into account the actual variations in teacher approach or student response that Cheryl now began to see in classroom encounters.

In our October 7, 1986, meeting, Cheryl spoke about "how much she was learning already" in our explorations, and "how she was beginning to see teaching differently." She expressed amazement that the others in the group, who had more years of teaching experience than she, would even be interested in the search. She attributed her new learnings to what she characterized as her relative inexperience in the classroom, and she revealed a preconception about the stance of the experienced teacher:

> I don't think the teachers I know who have been teaching twenty years would want to do this. But maybe I'm wrong. Just like I can see how my own perceptions of doing research might not be the way it has to be. I can tell already that my original ideas for my study weren't as full as they are now. And I can also see how my teaching of the LD kids is changing already. I'm trying to work out ways for them to write more, to keep journals in our class. So that they can have more ways of responding than I have been providing. And this is hard, because writing is hard for these kids and they are so impulsive; it's hard to get some of them to concentrate for more than a minute. But they like the journals! . . . But it's hard for them and me, because I feel so constrained by all the testing that I have to do and by all the ways in which other people think you should teach these learning disabled kids.

Cheryl shared a few of her early teaching experiences in Israel, where she felt alone, not only because of her American accent in

49

Hebrew but also because she had no other teachers to whom she could turn for guidance or support. When she returned to the United States and started teaching learning disabled students in the Bronx, she wanted to teach well and to fit in with her colleagues. She then spoke of the ways in which her educational background, her concentration upon the behavior-oriented field of special education, and her desires to teach well among a community of colleagues had, in a sense, prevented her from questioning the standard teaching approaches in her field:

> My whole career in education, since I was a child, has been "spit back, spit back." As a student, give them the answers I think they wanted, or now, as a teacher, the ones I've been told the kids should have. And I'm very good at "spit back." I've learned a lot of material. But I don't ever think that I've had to think.
>
> But now, I think that I'm starting to think, and I'd like my students to be able to do that too. I don't want them to grow up and not be able to think. And I want to work with teachers who can think too, who can see what they're doing with kids that might help them to think instead of just "spitting back." It's hard in special education. They don't give you much room to move beyond.

In my November 5, 1986, journal response to Cheryl, I asked questions about the preparation of special education teachers, not only to compare or contrast their preparation with that of other classroom teachers but also to better understand Cheryl's sense of not having "much room to move beyond":

> I guess what I'm wondering about now is what kind of preparation do LD teachers get? Is there any attention paid to the kind of thing that you are trying to do with your students? How do LD teachers "measure" their own success? That is, in what ways do they conceptualize their work and the ways in which they acknowledge "knowing"? Do the preparation programs emphasize different ways of knowing? I would think that they would, given the special problems of learning disabled children, for example, and the different ways in which they have had to accomodate their learning processes. You, for example, are utilizing an aesthetic experience, the listening and responding to music, as a possible way for students to exhibit some ways in which they might "know" some things that cannot be articulated in "school" fashion. To what extent are LD teachers prepared to recognize and acknowledge the students' responses as perhaps a different way of knowing?

Cheryl Special Ed

As Cheryl and I wrote to each other, I learned a great deal about the work and preparation of LD teachers, and Cheryl began to question the frameworks that had guided her work thus far in her teaching career. Further, as our collaboration continued and as Cheryl shared her questions with the group, her research focus slowly turned from her students' questions and responses to the possible underlying structures that encouraged the "flat" responses that she and the other LD teachers often gave to the children.

Cheryl continued to research the interactions of students and teachers and to focus her journal upon her ongoing observations and interviews. As we moved through the first months of our collaboration, Cheryl's journal was filled with her questions about the extent of her own replication of the very processes that she was observing and critiquing in others. By her January 2, 1987, journal entry, Cheryl was framing her concerns within a slightly different research focus from the one with which she began:

> I am concerned with LD teachers' flexibility in allowing students to express themselves. Teacher preparation for LD teachers focuses on outcomes and not so much on processes, or alternative ways of knowing. They focus on secure, easily recognizable outcomes. I personally feel that in LD teaching, one needs to mix elements of direct teaching and keep very good records of what and how the kids do, while allowing alternatives in curriculum, testing, and ways of knowing. I want to interview LD teachers to find out ways in which they conceptualize their work, and ways in which they acknowledge their own and students' knowing.

Cheryl's concern for the limited nature of her LD students' responses led her to a deeper examination of those responses as a reflection of the interaction between teacher and student, rather than as reflection of students' deficiencies per se. This shifting focus also represents Cheryl's growing awareness of and discomfort with the "flat" modes of responses that typify a mechanistic approach to teaching and learning. Cheryl began to consider the possibility of alternative ways of knowing that she had not experienced in her own educational activities. She wanted to develop ways of working within her own classroom that could enable both her students and herself to see learning as more than "spit back."

The shifting and expanding of the "flat" dimensions of Cheryl's area of specialization and their attendant pedagogical approaches

51

continue to be the center of Cheryl's work as a researching teacher. She often steps back from her daily teaching procedures and contexts. Through her journal, our group meetings, and extensive conversations with the teachers with whom she works, Cheryl is beginning to identify some underlying assumptions that guide her work as well as that of other special educators. As she moves back into her daily teaching, she continues to acknowledge her discomfort with the heretofore taken for granted, and wants to look further into the guiding constructs of her work. Although in her journal and in our group meetings she focuses more on actual classroom interactions than on herself, Cheryl, like the rest of us, continues to grapple with connections as well as contradictions between our conceptions of teaching and research and the structures which guide those conceptions.

The Science Teacher and Mentor

In 1985, the New York State Education Department issued a new elementary science syllabus, and appointed seventy-two mentors from a variety of geographic areas within the state. These mentors were prepared by state representatives to present activity-based in-service workshops designed to involve teachers in the problem-solving processes that undergird the new syllabus. Marjorie was chosen as a mentor, based on her extensive science teaching experience. Although she had most recently taught science at the high school level for twelve years, and had a Master's degree in biological sciences, her undergraduate degree was in elementary education and she had taught at the kindergarten to eighth-grade level for five years prior to moving to the high school level.

Marjorie had participated in a two-week training session for mentors in midsummer 1986, during which the mentors were introduced to the problem-solving emphasis within the new elementary science curriculum as well as to the possible "change agent" potential within their roles as mentors. As we began our collaborative studies, Marjorie also was beginning the first of her series of in-service programs, and she chose these in-service experiences as her initial focus in our explorations.

Marjorie began her own journal at that two-week mentor training session. Her journal keeping was not framed by any attempt to formalize a research focus, such as Cheryl was attempting to do that summer. Rather it was an extension of our discussions about the possible formation and processes of a research group.

Her initial journal entries reflected her experiences at the summer workshop and especially pointed to the state's emphasis on a particular conception of these mentors as "change agents" (from an August 30, 1986, journal entry):

> I want to do more than implement this syllabus—I really want to change the way they think about themselves as teachers. Is this too ambitious a task? Will I do either or both a disservice in attempting to do so? Am I clear enough on each issue to even attempt it? Will my uncertainties undermine or free them? I will need a response to help give me direction—some teachers will want structure—"just tell me how to do this"—they're already insecure. How can I make them more so by encouraging "the mess"? Is their writing to be a key? What if they won't write? I can't make them.

Even within the context of the state-constructed parameters of the mentors' work, Marjorie's questions focused upon her own attempts to understand the possible role configurations of "change agent." Her concerns were focused on teachers and what Beth had called their "low self-esteem." Marjorie wanted to work with teachers rather than talk at them about the new syllabus; her questions pointed to her hesitant feelings about ways to "change the way they think about themselves as teachers." Her hesitations and questions led to the development of a major ongoing theme within our group's discussions and debates.

In our discussions with Marjorie about the state's approach to the development and implementation of this new science syllabus, we raised the possibility that what Paulo Freire (1974) calls "malefic generosity" could be embedded in self-identified or appointed change agents' approaches and intents. Freire warns of the subtle and often unconscious ways in which attempts to help others may become infused with unexamined assumptions about the "right" ways to be or to act. These "right" ways often reflect the attitudes and stances of those who are in charge, and who thus have power to decide, rather than represent the actual needs or desires of those identified as needing "help." Connected to the "deficit" model of teacher preparation and development, Freire's concept of "malefic generosity" illuminates the impositional and oppressive nature of many programs and approaches in education.

Examination of these concepts became a center not only of Marjorie's ongoing research but also of our group's explorations. As we began to examine our schooling experiences in light of deficit models and possible personal as well as institutional enactments of malefic generosity, Marjorie quickly began to question the ways in which the state education representatives expected the mentors to function. She shared some of her questions as well as her worries in our meeting of September 20, 1986:

> I have a lot of questions about my role, and they're not only about the way in which I think of myself as a change agent. Can I do any of it? And what is it?

In my excitement about our chosen research angle of teacher-as-researcher, I offered a suggestion for Marjorie's approach to her in-service workshops:

> Maybe you could set up with some of your teachers the same processes that we are doing here to examine teacher-as-researcher. Maybe that's how you could set up your workshops with them—have them become teacher/researchers.

Marjorie responded:

> I just don't see how I could have room to do that right now with them. The state workshops that we are leading are so totally prescriptive. Problem solving, which is the whole essence of the new syllabus—it's really hard to understand what problem solving means—to just get them inside of the whole concept of [problem solving, which is] what we're asking them to do with the kids. What I did this summer, with the six steps to the model that they gave us for problem solving, was that I took a discrepancy. Always a problem has to start with a discrepancy between what you expect and what is. In the syllabus, some of the discrepancies are set up and some occur naturally. But that's the whole origin of a problem to be solved. So, what I started to do this summer was to take a discrepancy that I was feeling between what they want us to do and what I felt, and make that my problem. Then I tried to analyze what was happening to me using the steps of the problem solving model.

Beth asked:

> Did you solve the problem differently than how they were telling you to solve it?

Marjorie responded:

> They're not asking us to solve a problem. They're just telling us, "do this." But
> I felt a discrepancy, so for me it was a problem. And I was trying to get inside
> of the concept of what it means to solve a problem. I just have a hunch that
> unless the teachers can do that too, they'll never really understand what they
> are being asked to do with this syllabus in the classroom.

In September, Marjorie began to observe another mentor who was experienced in presenting other state-prepared materials and approaches. As Marjorie watched this mentor present the new workshops in science for elementary teachers, her hunches were confirmed about teachers' needing to engage in the very problem-solving activities that they would present to their students (from a September 25, 1986, journal entry):

> Why is he spending so much time giving them information? He's lecturing
> and not letting them get into any of the problems. I think that he needs to
> encourage them that there's no one right way and then lead them into
> problem-solving and be sensitive to their questions. That one teacher who
> questioned him about losing control with the kids if you let them engage in
> the mess of problem solving—he missed a chance to engage with her by not
> pursuing this important question.

By introducing us to discrepancies and "the mess" as prerequisites of problem-solving, and by sharing her explorations of her felt discrepancies within her role as a state mentor, Marjorie provided us with some ways to frame the collaborative work that we were attempting. In her attempts to "get inside the problem-solving," she encouraged the rest of us to do the same with our new teacher-researcher stances. Marjorie particularly emphasized the importance of not moving too quickly from "the mess" of searching for sources of one's identified discrepancies. With this emphasis, she provided a conceptual balance for all of us who were struggling with the pressures of "having the right answers" or of feeling "pulled apart" or of feeling "out of place" with the mechanistic approaches and structures that girded many of the educational settings in which we worked.

As our collaboration developed during that autumn of 1986, Marjorie continued to focus on "the mess" that characterized her approaches to her work as mentor rather than on the predetermined outcomes that seemed to frame other mentors' conceptions of their roles as change agents. "The mess" for Marjorie included points of uneasiness and a simultaneous sense of comfort and familiarity with the prescriptive way in which the state mentors were to present the problem-solving model itself. Another "messy" layer developed as she actually began to conduct her in-service programs and was confronted by some of her in-service teachers' points of dissonance and resistance. Journal entries chronicled her struggle with discrepancies within her own assumptions about problem-solving, science teaching, and in-service contexts (from an October 28, 1986, journal entry):

> I find myself wondering about the teachers' lack of background. I'm comfortable with them letting kids "mess around" in trying to solve problems but I find myself wanting the teachers to be able to lead/channel their efforts to arrive at "correct concepts." I guess that I *do* believe that there are such things. I want to lead them to correct conclusions too—and yet I really don't want to limit them by what I perceive as correct. I think that this problem-solving model appeals to me because it provides a way out of total control by me (or them in the classroom). I know now that I always thought that I had to teach with total control. This prescriptive tendency in me is hard to look at now, harder to change. And yet we still *are* in control in some ways in the classroom, in leading inservice workshops. How then can I provide the background—the correct concepts? It seems like too much to teach them concepts *and* really get them to understand problem-solving. I'm feeling what teachers feel all the time, I guess. Does it have to be either/or?

As she looked at her own pedagogical assumptions within the new contexts of the in-service workshops as well as our collaboration, Marjorie wrote of her growing awareness of the ways in which her prescriptive approaches to teaching were deeply embedded. Yet she struggled with "the mess" of exploring the sources and structures that constantly reinforced those tendencies as the "correct ones" for teachers to assume. She continued to frame her struggles from her new perspective as mentor (from a November 13, 1986, journal entry):

> How can I get them to share more with me and with one another? It's important to me that they make their own connections. . . . Do I let [all] get what they will from our experiences or try to predetermine what they should get (in terms of what I think they'll need to teach problem-solving effectively)?

The difficulties of encouraging people to make their own connections, and at the same time, of teaching them mandated versions of content and process, emerged as a predominant theme in Marjorie's continuing in-service work. It also has become an important point in our examinations of possibilities for emancipation within the teacher-as-researcher construct. In a certain sense, we still are in "the mess" of examining the underlying sources of the various contradictions that characterize our educational roles as well as trying to act in ways that change or eliminate those contradictions. We still meet because these resolutions are difficult and the changes come slowly.

Marjorie alluded to the possibilities of getting through this extended "messy stage" in an example from an in-service workshop in which some teachers had been particularly resistant (from a January 29, 1987, journal entry):

> The resistant group got involved in spite of themselves when they discovered a non-symmetrical ping-pong ball that bounced differently depending on where it hit! It was their problem and they experienced a need to know that had not/could not occur (given their resistance) in response to problems that I had posed. I pointed this out to them—I don't think they were really ready to hear what I was saying but it was a great demonstration for me of people getting from/learning what they want from an experience. Teachers can't determine lesson objectives alone! When these teachers got involved, they were actually dealing with the same broad concept that I was trying to engage them in—but it happened when they were free to buy in, to make their own connections.

By identifying one point of dissonance, that of a sense of incongruence between what she was to do as a science mentor and how she was to do it as determined by others, and by making that discrepancy the focus of her own research, Marjorie began to model that process of reflection and action for her in-service teachers. In a dialogue from March 14, 1987, she shared the effects of that sharing and modeling:

> One teacher in my group got permission to hold a science fair in his class. He used some of the approaches with his students that he had learned in my workshop. Through his kids' work, he was modeling the problem solving for other students as well as for other teachers in the school. He went about establishing his own version of the science fair; the other teachers saw what

he was doing, and just like the kids, they got interested in the process and the possibilities. Through his own problem solving, he moved past potential problems with peer resentment, with distrust of the other teachers in his role as an outreach agent of this inservice in problem solving. I think that he ended up empowering himself as well as some other teachers; it just didn't stay with himself. That's the best of what this teacher-as-researcher can do.

Marjorie worried because not many in-service teachers responded to her invitation to become teacher-researchers with her in the context of their work together. Those who did respond did not appear to participate as our group did. However, this one example of the teacher who acted on his own, within the contexts of his understandings of problem solving and of the relationships between teaching and research, represents the strengths and possibilities that exist when we allow ourselves to acknowledge and begin with "the mess."

Marjorie's attempts to research and to act on her own discrepancies continue to motivate the members of our collaborative group to pursue our explorations and to remain in "the mess." It is an uncomfortable feeling to be in the center of the mess; but within our collaborative work, we have begun to see the importance of its ferment. Remaining in the mess provides us with one way to resist the pressure of "correct" and "prescriptive" stances within our collaboration as well as within our individual educator roles.

Writing theorist and researcher Ann Berthoff (1987a) argues that research means looking and looking again. This conception of research requires that we resist the urge to leave the mess for promises of certainty and closure. It requires that we try to get inside, as Marjorie did in her attempts to understand the concept of problem-solving, and once there, to "look and look again." Remaining in "the mess," as Marjorie encouraged us to do, is analogous to "learning the uses of chaos" that Berthoff argues is a necessary part of both writing and research processes. In our collaboration, we have found comfort in Berthoff's corollaries for learning the uses of chaos: Tolerate ambiguity and be patient with beginnings.

The Professor

As a result of the other group members' willingness to grapple with "the mess" stirred up by our investigations into the limits and emancipatory possibilities of teacher-as-researcher, I was able to begin looking and looking again at my major discrepancy thus far in the study. Throughout our work, I had talked and worried about imposing my conceptions upon the group members, and yet had struggled to understand the ways in which my voice, my concerns as professor and as originator of the invitation, could be relational and changing and, thus, not reified as "authoritative discourse."

As we moved through the initial months of our collaboration, I realized that, like Beth, I had assumed that my role required that I have the "right" answers, and that, like Kevin and Katherine, I felt "pulled apart" by this unexamined expectation of myself. As Cheryl began to explore the "flat" dimensions of teachers' responses to students, including her own, as a discrepancy, and as Marjorie continued her research by attempting to get inside the sources of her identified discrepancy between prescription and the "messing around" stage of problem solving, I began to see that I could not determine the research agendas or procedures for these people, even if I overtly tried to. In my concern over imposing the authority of my role and in my simultaneous struggle to believe in the authority of my own voice, I had come close to dismissing or ignoring or not seeing the active agency of these people with whom I was working. These educators were quite capable of determining and exploring the issues that they wished to investigate, and, in fact, did not look to me for approval or direction as they grappled with their discrepancies. They did, however, bring those struggles to our collaboration, and in their sharing, I was only one among the group who could offer response and discussion. I had to look and look again in order to begin to see the irony embedded within my understandings of my role, even as I supposedly worked toward "emancipatory enactments" of teaching, research, and collaboration between university and classroom teachers.

Throughout my initial dialogue journal exchanges with my co-researchers are examples of my apologies and worries about being too directive, too formative in my approach or my expectations for our work together. And yet I now see that I had an underlying expectation for myself as professor, as the convenor of this group, that conformed to traditional conceptions of leader within that role (an excerpt from my September 21, 1986, journal entry):

I'm really nervous about the ways in which I introduced the whole idea of teacher-as-researcher to the group. I talk like I know what I'm doing, but of course I don't. And I try to tell that to them too, but they all look at me, to me. "Why else would we be here?" I'm sure that's what they are thinking. Hope that they didn't feel pressure to have to decide what they were going to focus upon in their research, at least right away. How much am I able to "let things emerge," as I always recommend for others?

My fears continued to emerge in our meetings and in our dialogue journal writing (from a November 11, 1986, response to Katherine):

I am very nervous about these things that I point to because I am afraid that I am attempting to put too much framework around us or that I am misinterpreting or not seeing everything that is going on (expectations for myself—hard on myself, like you).

At our December 1, 1986, meeting, Katherine brought up my expectation that I "had to see it all." As the group talked about the impossibility and undesirability of that expectation, I tried to unravel my sense of "feeling so responsible" for the group, and to talk about ways in which those responsible feelings could get contorted into controlling or manipulative behavior. As I was struggling through this, Katherine asked, "Without you, would we still meet?" This was not a question that soothed my anxieties. I tried to sort through my responses:

From my perspective, I feel as though you are my co-learners in all of this, you know, co-researchers. And yet there's a way in which I fear that you are just doing this to please me because you still see me as teacher, even though we aren't in classes together anymore. See, I think everyone here is perfectly capable of assuming the role that I have here, which is still sort of major responder to everyone's journal writing, for example. So, here I am, writing back to a psychologist, or a math chair, or a first-grade teacher, for pity's sake. You all know a lot more than I do about child psychology or math or special education, and I'm afraid that when I write back to you that maybe I haven't addressed or don't even get the issues that concern you. But then, I figure that you would tell me. I do trust you all that way.

Beth responded:

This is a new role for me, a new position to be in to be open with a teacher. I still see you as our teacher and yet I am beginning to see you more as a person here too, a friend. I actually have to work at it, feeling comfortable with the ambiguity of my feelings about your role. I always did want to please my teachers. I fight the feelings that come up when we ask, would we do this if you weren't here? Wanting to be a part of this so much, and yet worrying always about what happens next. That's my teacher part coming out.

Marjorie responded in turn:

I think that we like each other enough and get so much out of this that we would probably still come together. But you gave us a concrete purpose or reason for coming together, and I don't think that's bad or controlling. Somebody has to do that, or at least be able to say that there's a reason or maybe a discrepancy [laughter] that we should look at together. I don't think that necessarily puts everything on you.

I continued to struggle aloud:

Maybe I'm just afraid to take responsibility for this. And it takes the guise of "I don't want to intrude or impose." When, in fact, yea, it was my idea, and I'm really interested in this, and I think it has lots of potential for all kinds of educators and settings [I begin to talk faster here, and the group begins to laugh]. And also I have certain things I want to look at because I think there are important issues to work through in what we are doing, and so, you're right, I'm not admitting that as much as I should here. I have serious research interests here, and maybe I'm afraid to impose because I'm afraid of being self-serving. But I am really committed to us and to our processes. That's as honest as I can be right now.

My own explorations of the teacher-as-researcher construct, then, included my gradually giving up expectations for myself as the primary interpreter of our collective as well as individual experiences. I also began examining these expectations as replicating the very conceptions of teaching, research, curriculum, and collaboration that maintain inequitable and voiceless relations among teachers, administrators, students. The December meeting in which the group members pressed me to consider my underlying assumptions about my role within our collaboration was a turning point for me. I continue to grapple with this discrepancy, for even though I work within conceptual frameworks that challenge such conceptions, I continue to find within myself examples of deeply embedded hierarchical assumptions about appropriate academic role and demeanor.

What has helped me in my attempts to uncover and to change these embedded preconceptions are the interactions and dialogues of

61

our group: together, we have created meanings and connections. Thus, I have realized that I do not need to do all the creating, nor do I have to remain on the edges of the spaces watching others create. Together, we have worked and reworked our perceptions of our separate and collective projects, not only in terms of individual problems and questions, but also in light of others' interpretations of the personal as well as the collective intentions and forms of our collaboration.

By the end of our first half-year of work together, we had begun to trace the underlying expectations, fears, conflicts, and questions that framed our collective and individual research. This tracing contributed to the unraveling of the seams that ordinarily pieced together the layers of our experience, of our daily lives as educators. The unraveling allowed points of dissonance to emerge, and, as we moved into a more comfortable understanding of our relationships to one another, we also began to address in detail the points of dissonance that emerged in our investigations. We wanted to focus on "what we could do," as Katherine said, and, at the same time, we knew that we were entering into the most difficult part of our work. As Kevin noted in our December meeting, "This is a real opportunity for us to find out what's really going on. We can't stop now." And so we continued to press, to look beneath our assumptions to the sources of our expectations as educators and to the forces that influence and frame those expectations. We wanted to understand, for ourselves and for our students, "what's really going on."

CHAPTER THREE

Emerging Constraints and Possibilities

As we moved through the formative aspects of our collaboration, we began to settle comfortably into our meetings and dialogues. These meetings and our dialogue journals during the first year allowed each of us to explore individual discrepancies and to share our questions. However, we still tended to discuss our individual senses of discrepancy as purely personal and idiosyncratic examples of the stresses and complexities of being educators. We needed to tell our own stories first, in order not only to establish our individual interests within our explorations but also to develop the trust to which Katherine alluded as she described her hesitations in writing.

As we shared and explored our individual educational situations and began to identify the discrepancies we faced in our work, we also began to develop an awareness of and respect for one another's struggles. As we invited each other to listen and respond to our individual stories, we also began to develop a trust in the accepting and supportive nature of our meetings and interactive journals. These elements appear to be necessary foundations for establishing collaborative approaches to examining the relationships among our personal perspectives, our situations, and both the diminishing and enabling dynamics of the contexts in which we work. We only began to look at these dimensions as we developed connections to one another and began to note the similarities and differences among our assumptions and school situations.

However, although we were meeting as a group, in that first year we still did not directly address our assumptions about the meanings, forms, and dimensions of collaboration. Nor did we immediately attempt to ascertain the role of collaboration within emancipatory forms of research and teaching. Rather, we came together in that first year as educators who shared similar concerns and questions about teaching and research. As we moved through our first year, we finally began to feel comfortable in questioning and pushing one another just a bit, in our effort to consider how our private and public worlds intersected. Through these interactions, we began to acknowledge both our separateness and our connectedness, and thus also began to consider the problems and potentials of collaborative studies.

That December meeting was pivotal for several reasons. Kevin's desire to "find out what's really going on" reflected a developing intent among us all. We were beginning to confront the discrepancies in our own situations, and in so doing, to see the ways in which our various situations contributed to the similarities and differences among us. The group began to coalesce, not in terms of similar perspectives or identified discrepancies, but in the work of exploring those intersections of our public and private worlds.

As part of our collaboration, we shared our growing understandings of our own and one another's situations and discrepancies. We also began to encourage one another to find spaces in our daily lives to try to act, at least in small initial ways, upon the givens we had internalized about our educational roles and functions. This meant that we had to look and look again at the sources of our unexamined assumptions about teaching, research, curriculum, the functions of schools, and the relationships among them. Then, through this examination, we thought we might begin to question those givens that we felt were undermining our action within these relationships. To even call into question the givens was a form of often painful action for each of us.

The action implied in "finding out what's really going on" continues to be the most difficult aspect of our collaborative efforts. Yet we are convinced that this is the crucial point in concretizing the possibilities of critical and emancipatory teaching and research. Within the first half-year of our explorations, we already had identified aspects of our educational roles and settings which we felt persistently blocked or limited us in acting as challengers.

These inhibiting elements became repeated themes in our discussion and writing, and continued to emerge in various forms throughout our developing explorations.

Themes and Variations

At this point, I want to present the themes of time, of multiple layers, and of uncertainties so that readers might then trace their reappearances and variations throughout our evolving collaboration. The group feels that these themes represent obstacles, both internal and external, to emancipatory teaching and research within the daily lives of educators. At the same time, we also point out the ways in which we are attempting to deal with these as obstacles to be overcome rather than as total obstructions to our purposes. We are looking for ways in which to see these themes and variations from a variety of angles so that we are not trapped in habitual responses to these seemingly perpetual blocks to reflexive and critical inquiry. These ways are unique to the individuals within our group, and so cannot provide prescriptions or even guidelines for action; however, they do exemplify educators' struggles within a variety of school settings, and therefore may provide insight and encouragement, or at least a sense of possible connections among those readers who wish to engage in similar investigations.

Time

Throughout the initial months of our collaboration, issues of time emerged in a variety of forms and levels of meaning in our discussions and writings.

Time issues, in fact, dominated the formative months of our work. We had, and continue to have, difficulties in arranging mutually agreeable meeting times. We live in far-flung locations, and each of us must drive an hour or more to our meetings, depending on the location for that specific gathering. Our teaching and administrative schedules often conflict; I teach my graduate classes in the evening, and the other group members teach or counsel or administer during regular school hours. Often we meet in the evening, after I have taught a class and after others have worked a full school day and have themselves taken graduate classes. Sometimes, we meet on week-ends, and most often, the last part of each meeting is devoted to juggling schedules in order to arrange the next meeting time for us all.

Most of us find it difficult to write in our journals in a daily or regular way. When we engage in dialogue journal writing, we find the time lapses between our responses tend to vary, depending on our other personal and professional obligations.

As Katherine most strongly noted, she found it difficult to find the time not only to write but also to think and reflect during her daily teaching routine. Although Kevin could find some times within his counseling schedule to jot notes to himself, these mostly focused on his clients' responses and behaviors rather than on his own reactions or feelings within those counseling sessions. Kevin still has to find the time outside of his daily schedule and obligations to do his own journal writing. Cheryl, Beth, Marjorie, and I all tend to do our writing in the early morning hours, before the press of work and family obligations closes around us. Many of our dialogue journal entries begin with early morning times noted in the margin. But in some way, this has established another connective dimension for us. As I noted in one of my entries to Cheryl, "I don't feel so lonely if I know you are up writing too at these crazy hours." Marjorie and I especially are fond of writing journal entries on backs of envelopes and scraps of paper as we scribble notes to ourselves during workshops or teaching activities. We all have been known to staple such scraps into our "real" journals, for we neither feel the need nor have to time to reenter these thoughts as completed pieces.

Each of us has to carve time out of existing schedules to meet, to reflect, to write, if we so choose. We are, in a sense, still trying to create the kinds of space "where dialogue can take place and freedom can appear." These spaces, we have come to realize, must be literal as well as figurative; our collaboration requires a commitment of time, and a subsequent reordering of priorities for each of us so that we can meet together, not only in spirit but in literal community.

There also are ways in which time collapses and expands in our collective space, once we are able to gather together. We still are seeking the forms and processes by which we may share our work as well as move forward, in both our thinking and our doing. We are gentle and attentive in the sharing and shaping of our time together. We still offer each other the openings in which to speak, to debate, to question, and, although our conversations are quite often lively and full of a "sense of urgency," to quote a phrase from Katherine, they also are often slow and filled with silence. None of us rushes to fill those spaces; it is as though we have come to understand the necessary disjunctures between the temporal reality that we are sharing and the inner time of each of us. We all respond to one another, to our situations, and to our explorations at different times and in separate rhythms. There is no attempt by any of us to force a synchronous relationship among our individual inner times, and in that unspoken understanding, our silences have meaning.

These silences are important, too, in that they balance that sense of urgency that often results when our clock time together is so limited. It is difficult to resist premature conclusions and directions and prescriptions for action in our work together, but often our silent reflections prevent those closures.

Each time that we meet, we are amazed by how time disappears and simultaneously unfolds. We continue to note, over time, how the directions of our work as well as the definitions and understandings of our research and collaboration are changing. We are realizing how much time we need to reconsider, to confront, to excavate. We continue to carve out the time that allows us to look and look again, because, as Cheryl noted in our February 2, 1987, meeting, our time together helps us gather strength to keep going.

Multiple Layers

In the initial phases of our work together, we told and retold our individual stories as a way of making connections with one another. These stories also provided a background against which we could begin to examine, from various angles, the interwoven nature of our public and private worlds. The multiple stories were a natural response as we came to know one another as pursuing the possibilities inherent in viewing ourselves as educators-researchers. The stories that we shared about ourselves as part of our collaborative processes also had the potential to keep us from being captured, as Grumet (1987) warned, by a single narrative. The very nature of our long-term collaboration has prevented such static portraits or prescriptions of teacher-as-researcher. It has simultaneously allowed the weaving together of our stories into layers of constantly shifting connections among us. These developing stories and our collective and changing narratives belie the completed stories that are frozen by a distanced and "objective" researcher's glance.

Thus, as we told our stories and worked not only to find "evidence of the external forces that have diminished us" but also to "recover our own possibilities," we began to move through some of the layers of our assumptions that overlay our daily actions. A further obstacle that emerged in our explorations of this theme was another assumption, shared by each of us at one time or another in our work: once we had addressed an issue or peeled back a layer of embedded expectation, we somehow thought that we had worked through that layer, believed we had removed enough of the constraints of our assumptions to eliminate the layer itself. We constantly caught ourselves being captured by a single reflection of ourselves within one narrative, within one situation we thought we had moved beyond and therefore had completed. We should not have been surprised, and yet we almost always were, when the same layer reappeared weeks or months later, wrapped around our conversations or our examples of our latest researching efforts.

At the same time, as we addressed the layers of our assumptions and worked to move through them to another plane from which we might see "further and bigger," as Kevin put it, we also created layers of possibilities for ourselves to work in new ways. This simultaneous sifting through and rebuilding of our assumptions surrounding our work as educators is intertwined with the obstacle of time; both the peeling and the reconstructing of layers are ongoing and long-term efforts, in the temporal sense, and contradict the end-product emphasis within which most of us do our daily work.

As part of these simultaneous processes, some of the group members wanted to replicate, in various ways, the approaches to teacher-as-researcher that we were developing together. This replication perhaps could create, we thought, another layer of experience within which we could examine diminishing forces as well as possibilities for change for ourselves. for our students, and for others with whom we work.

For example, when Kevin shifted his focus from his high school clients to his elementary school setting, he not only began to write about his own "pulled apart" feelings in that setting but also began to consider having his elementary school students use journal writing in their counseling sessions. He was nervous about this decision for several reasons. First of all, Kevin never had used journal writing with these second-through-sixth-grade children, and he was unsure not only of their writing capabilities but also of how to introduce and sustain the children's writing in the counseling sessions. Secondly, he was unclear if this added process within his counseling repertoire would be of benefit to the children or to himself as a psychologist or could help him continue to examine the underlying sources of his "pulled apart" feelings within his institutional setting.

Furthermore, although he had used children's drawings to complement his counseling techniques, he had drawn upon research in his field and had consulted the standard references as he worked with his clients' drawings. There was little if any research in elementary counseling on the use of children's writing as a therapeutic tool, and he worried in our February 2, 1987, meeting, "what if I see nothing in the kids' writing, or even if I do, what if I don't know what to do with it?"

The idea that he could be a creator, a researcher of his own practice, was one that still scared not only Kevin but the rest of us as well. As much as we were working to understand the emancipatory aspects of our own research and practice, and as much as that required that we view ourselves as creators, as active agents, we all still found ourselves relying on and returning to the very layers of other-determined research and practice that we were attempting to challenge.

As Kevin discussed his worries about this latest refocusing of his research, he talked about his initial efforts to introduce writing into his counseling sessions with some of the elementary school children:

> What I've been doing is that I've been asking them to write as part of the counseling session. Some of them have really taken to it, and some of them have really been resistant. One especially has really resisted, and so I have backed off on the writing with him altogether. I think it would have been different if I had introduced this with him at the beginning of our relationship, but I have been seeing him for four months now, and I think that it's too abrupt a change in our counseling routine for him. Maybe I can work it in very slowly with him.

As he talked, Kevin then recalled his own resistance and fear of writing at the beginning of our collaboration. Through the course of our work thus far, Kevin had developed into a prolific journal writer, and his reasons for wanting to try the journal writing as a tool within his counseling were based on his own positive experiences. However, his nervousness surrounding his attempts to introduce journal writing into his work with elementary school students brought to the surface again a layer of apprehension about his own writing and his use of it in counseling. That apprehension, in turn, resurrected Beth's questions about the "right way of doing this" and the reasons for Katherine's reluctance to write at all. As we worked through these resurfacing anxieties at this meeting, we all, in one way or another, began to acknowledge the halting and undulating nature of our quest to become challengers. The layers of uncertainty about both our own capabilities and the appropriate directions of our research explorations simultaneously unfolded and closed around us.

Kevin talked about one way in which he thought he might be able to examine the uses of journal writing with elementary school clients as well as continue to pursue the sources of his own fragmented feelings in the school:

> I was thinking that maybe I could include in my research the writing that the kids do in their classrooms. I think that as a school psychologist, much more than a psychologist in private practice, I have real access to what happens with these kids in the classroom. And most of the kids that I see, many of their problems are reflected in the classroom. That's why I'm usually seeing them, because of references from their teachers. And it also brings the teacher into it, and maybe that could be a link for me in trying to see the bigger sources in the structure of the school and why I feel as I do there. I just think that this could provide a link for me, a way of interacting with the teachers that might shed some light on a lot of things, not only these kids' problems, that I might explore more fully by having them write.

Marjorie also was attempting to replicate some of our processes by having her in-service teachers do some journal writing as part of the "messing around" of problem-solving. She wasn't finding much response among her teachers, and she attributed some of this resistance to the relatively short-term nature of the eight-week in-service program. Yet, Marjorie, like Kevin, felt that involving the teachers with whom she was working in some of the processes of our collaboration might provide a link, as Kevin said, between our work and the larger world. Marjorie wanted to examine the sources of these teachers' resistance as another way of looking "further and bigger" into the constraints as well as possibilities of emancipatory conceptions of teaching and research. She, like Kevin and Cheryl, who also was doing dialogue journal writing with several of her LD teacher colleagues, was attempting to build a layer of conceptual understandings in her teachers as much as she was trying to work through the existing layers of resistance in them. As she realized in our February 2 meeting, she also found barriers within herself:

> I want to get to some of the deeper issues with the in-service that I'm doing with the state syllabus. And as we talk, I see a layer for myself here. I'm doing a lot of short-term work, and am starting from scratch with all different groups of teachers. And it's like I'm always beginning again, and I've taken a lot of notes, but I was really getting frustrated because the teachers weren't doing the writing like I thought they should.
>
> Last Tuesday, I had a real nice in-service session, and Janet said to me, "did you write?" And I just thought, well there's nothing to write about, it's the same stuff. It's the first session, it's the second session, and nothing's happening yet. I'll write again when we start getting into something. And then I thought, well, I didn't feel guilty. [Laughter here, as I interjected, "Oh, great, now I feel guilty because I made you do this!"] No, it was just a reminder that I really want to do this. And how could I be upset with my teachers for not writing if I didn't! So I sat down to write.
>
> I'm doing two simultaneous workshops—it's like having the same class twice—so I wrote down notes of what I was doing. As I did that, it started to trigger questions. I reflected on the questions, and by the time I was done, I realized that there was a lot more there than I had ever considered there might be. I had thought that it would only be the same old beginning stuff. I see that I was assuming the same thing that you are worried about, Kevin, that there might not be anything there. But once I got into it, obviously, there's a whole lot now for me to think about.

Our layers of assumptions, particularly surrounding our conceptions of knowledge as determined by someone else's research, constantly resurface within our explorations. None of us had any predetermined guidelines or traditional research evidence to support our own researching attempts. We could admit that we wanted such guidelines or evidence not only to provide new knowledge about in-service or counseling techniques, for example, but also to provide new knowledge about ourselves as researching educators and about our appropriate relationships to our research participants and processes. However, we also knew such research goals were beyond the bounds of standard educational research methodology or researcher stance, and, as such, created uneasiness and another layer of apprehension within each of us. Beth's question, "Are we doing this right?" surfaced repeatedly. Given our years of accepting research as "objective" and of seeing ourselves as transmitters rather than creators of knowledge, we agreed that we had reason to worry that "there might not be anything there" if we were the only ones doing the looking.

However, as we all pushed to become challengers in our teaching and researching efforts, we were constantly surprised by how many questions we could generate and how many contexts we could examine, once we considered ourselves as appropriate generators of those questions and examinations. To look and look again allowed us to realize that, as Marjorie said, "there's a lot more there than I had ever considered there might be." This centering process, however, required constant vigilance, for we all were accustomed to having others, in authoritative voices and official positions, tell us both the appropriate questions and the correct answers.

Further, there often were no spaces outside our collective in which such teacher-generated research was encouraged or acknowledged as legitimate. Thus, we not only had to confront our own layers of assumptions in attempting to become creators of knowledge but also had to address the question of how we might deal with the layers of assumptions that covered other educators' perceptions of appropriate production of research and officially sanctioned knowledge. We were becoming acutely aware of what Zeichner and Liston (1987) had noted in their attempts to teach student teachers to reflect: typical schooling contexts do not encourage or welcome teachers' involvement in inquiry and reflection upon their work.

We were confronting the layers of hierarchical organization that tended to separate and classify individuals, and we also were beginning to see the ironies inherent in attempting to become challengers within such frameworks:

> Even when practitioners, educators, and researchers question the model of technical rationality, they are party to institutions that perpetuate it. . . . Researchers are supposed to provide the basic and applied science from which to derive techniques for diagnosing and solving the problems of practice. Practitioners are supposed to furnish researchers with problems for study and with tests of the utility of research results. The researcher's role is distinct from, and usually considered superior to, the role of the practitioner. (Schön 1983, 26)

The standard separation of researcher and practitioner roles to which Schön refers confounded our efforts to conceive of research as *praxis* and to participate in the reciprocal and negotiated relationships that such a concept requires. Even as we attempted these relationships among ourselves, part of our work together involved our struggle to even understand how to create negotiated and reciprocal positions within our collaborative framework. These difficulties were compounded when we had to confront, usually individually and in isolation from our collaborative group, those layers of the educational community's expectations and requirements for our separate roles as researchers or practitioners.

Thus, we continue to work through the layers of our own expectations for ourselves as researchers and practitioners; we try to note the ways in which our expectations and difficulties are shaped by the complex relationships among the forces of power, control, prediction, and accountability that drive much of current educational research and practice. We also try to see the spaces within and among these relationships where we can take action to change the inequitable or silencing effects of those forces on ourselves and on the students and colleagues with whom we work.

Our changing conceptions of the processes of research as well as of our participation in those processes reflect most immediately the simultaneous unfolding and reconstructing of the layers that influence our work together. We were beginning to see, in the first year of our explorations, the ways in which what each of us did in our daily work as teacher, as administrator, or as psychologist could be regarded as a form of research. We had begun with a hunch that we all were searching for ways to create connections among the contents, processes and situations with and in which we and our colleagues work. None of us could have said, in the beginning of our collaboration, that we understood research to contain the possibility of joint constructions of meaning. Nor could we have articulated the ways in which those joint constructions could challenge the structures of schooling that deny our voices or our potentials as knowers in the world. We were only beginning to understand those potentials as we worked through our first year of collaboration. Through our struggles to identify and restructure the layers of expectations and requirements surrounding our roles as educators, we were slowly starting to consider Freire's (1985) concept of research as tapping sources of knowledge not previously recognized as legitimate.

We discussed our changing understanding of research at our February 2, 1987, meeting. We focused on the difficulties of believing in our own capabilities and voices as educators-researchers and of confronting the structures that reinforced our insecurities. Beth, who had applied for and been chosen as her school district's evaluator, was struggling with the dimensions of her decision to leave the classroom and to enter full-time administrative work. She asked:

> Could my job as district evaluator be the kind of research that we are attempting? How can I evaluate programs, and the people who are the programs, and still involve them in the negotiating and participating in research that we talk about here?

Marjorie replied:

> Well, you can start out by situating yourself in the research, and pointing out your perspective to them. You can acknowledge that you have a perspective. You know, you could talk to them about the fact that everyone has a viewpoint, and that you are interested in their viewpoint of a program or a curriculum or whatever it is that you are evaluating. We're just so conditioned to do what's expected of us, even in research.

In our discussion, layers of conditioning, as Marjorie called it, surfaced as we tried to talk about possible new definitions of research that were emerging in our work. At the same time, we did not want to lapse into definitive approaches or intentions for our work that would replicate the static nature of the very model of research that we wanted to challenge. We saw that there was no immediate threat of this, however, as we struggled just to clarify the ways in which our perceptions of the forms and functions of research were changing. I asked:

> How have your conceptions of research changed, if at all, based on our work thus far? I guess I don't mean to indicate that you've moved from one definition to another but just, what has happened thus far? We're not done, by any means. In fact, I still feel like we're just beginning. But I guess my question really is, do you feel like you are doing research?

Marjorie responded:

> I guess I feel a little more inside it, inside of the research process. Sort of like I tried to do with the problem-solving, to get inside of that concept to really

understand it. That's what research is for me now. When we started this project, I was reading a lot about teacher constructs. I was trying to figure out whose model I should use as I began my in-service work. But now I don't feel comfortable with others' models. I thought that I had to fit into someone else's structure. But now I want to develop my own way of looking at these teachers and our work together. But it's still scary. I'm sure someone is going to say to me, so what?

Katherine picked up on Marjorie's thoughts about having to use someone else's structures or models in research and, as Katherine noted, in teaching too:

I think that my idea of research has definitely changed. My idea before was that you had to find your backup in books, and you had to find sources that would back up any statement that you made. You had to back it up with something else that has already been established. Now I can definitely see what we're doing as research, only we're starting from scratch, and it's almost pure in a sense. I never really felt before that it was O.K. to start from scratch. Research was just using someone else's work to support what you were saying or doing in the classroom. Now maybe we could support ourselves. It's so personal that it makes it meaningful now.

Kevin expanded on this personal dimension:

It's much more internal than I thought it was going to be—our work together and research. Sometimes I'm afraid that I might not be out there enough, you know, that I might be too introspective in what I'm doing with my research, with the writing and the elementary kids. It—research—really is much more personal, like Katherine says, than I ever thought could be possible. But I like doing my own research. It helps me feel like I'm my own person, and that's always been really important to me. I think that people in education will start to feel more confident if they were to participate in something like this. I see more now.

With Katherine's and Kevin's comments about their surprise at the personal dimensions of research, we started to talk about our various experiences both as students and as teachers that negated this personal element we were finding within our research efforts. None of us, as students or teachers, had been encouraged to view our learning or teaching as a form of research, as a way of looking and looking again at what and how we wanted to find out about teaching and learning. As Cheryl had noted, we had become, in fact, quite adept at recycling the knowledge that had been presented to us in various classrooms throughout our lives. Thus these layers of experiences and expectations of ourselves as recipients, or, at best, dispensers of knowledge, continued to intermittently obscure the connections that we were beginning to make between the public and private aspects of teaching and research.

Beth spoke about the thickness of these layers, particularly as they covered her new job as the district evaluator:

> As I hear the rest of you talk about research, all I can say now is what it is not for me. And I know that if I tried to replicate what we're doing with a group of teachers now, I'd still go right to the structure that I first thought that we'd follow here. You know that I thought that we would get together and identify some issues that we wanted to research in our classrooms. I thought that we'd narrow them down to three or so, you know, like you get to vote on in-service topics, and then we'd go research those individually and then come back and discuss them. I'm still looking for this structure.
>
> And I got scared when we started to deviate from this. I got nervous that we weren't doing this right, as you all well know! [We laughed together, as Beth rolled her eyes during this statement.] I'm afraid that this has to do with feeling that I've only been successful when I've had structure. To let go of this might mean that I'd fall apart.
>
> But I see, now that we're pretty far into this, that I'm not falling apart. I have to fight my feelings of wanting a conclusion or an answer. In our research, I'm starting to see that there are no endings.

Cheryl responded to Beth's struggle:

> You know, we've really changed the purposes of research as we traditionally have known them. We all are doing this for ourselves and for the kids. And for the problems that we face in the classroom or wherever we work. We're not doing this because anyone told us that we had to, and we are not following anyone else's interests. And so I feel, anyway, that when I'm confronted every day with the structure of teaching LD kids (and there's lots of structure in the curriculum, in how we're supposed to work with them) that I can interrupt my patterns more easily now. I can see a little bit more how I get stuck in the structure. And I'm more willing to try to move out, to get unstuck.

I spoke of the layers of expectation and reward in academe that reinforced the still predominant modes of quantitative and prescriptive educational research. These layers influenced my graduate students' approaches to research as well as my own work as I attempted to participate in alternative forms of curriculum inquiry:

If you think about your traditional graduate research courses, you never see the mess of it, never much get to consider how the problems were originally identified or get to know the people who raised the original questions. I think that we are seeing each others' messes and conflicting notions, and we're watching each other wondering. It helps me to wonder more; I can at least say that.

Although our expectations about the appropriate intentions and methods of research perhaps reveal most directly the embedded as well as constantly changing layers of our understandings, we continue to find examples of this motif and its variations in all aspects of our explorations. It is in this sense that we all have noted, at one time or another, that we "aren't finished yet."

Uncertainties

The third theme, uncertainties, is interwoven among those of time and layers. It reveals itself also in our simultaneous movements toward and away from the issues and situations that we are attempting to address. As we work to unravel as well as to create, we often feel uncertain, not only about the possibilities of becoming challengers but also about the very work of recovering our own possibilities. As Cheryl noted, "It's just sometimes easier to pull the covers up over your head!"

Some of our uncertainties have to do with the procedures and forms of our collaborative work. Others are connected to our grapplings with the personal dimensions that permeate every aspect of our researching attempts. As Katherine and Kevin noted, nothing in their educational experience had prepared them for the thus far private, yet unsettling, discrepancies within their educator roles that their own researching efforts already had elicited. Further, the contexts in which we all worked heightened our uncertainties, for those contexts often denied the personal as an appropriate perspective from which to do that work. In struggling to acknowledge the dialectic of the personal and the public, we were feeling the loss of familiar layers of authority and position within which we had wrapped ourselves for so many years. As Cheryl noted, "you can really feel lonely thinking about these things."

At the same time, we all found it difficult to confront, on a daily basis, the contradictions and discrepancies that we found in our work as educators. The layers of traditional pedagogical and research frameworks sometimes appeared too substantial, too locked into place, to be challenged by our quiet questions. Sometimes it felt easier to deny those questions and to pull covers of conformity even tighter around us. However, our collaboration encouraged us to keep looking, and to acknowledge that, as Marjorie noted, "lots of what we're dealing with now are not new conflicts, really. It's just that now we can no longer deny them."

Marjorie continued to confront what she had identified as her prescriptive tendencies in her teaching and in-service efforts. Yet she felt uncertain about the content versus process debate every time she presented her science syllabus workshops. She had discussed these feelings of uncertainty with us many times, and in our March 2, 1987, meeting, she still was wrestling with this issue:

> I still think that there are certain ways that the teachers should do this problem-solving, even though I know that the root of problem-solving points to no one answer or correct way of doing it. So much of my science teaching, especially with the high school kids, focused on getting the right answer. I get discouraged sometimes when I keep finding this tendency in myself. And yet, sometimes, there are such things as right answers, don't you think?

Katherine, whose uncertainties about the journal writing aspects of our collaborative work were apparent in the initial phases, connected her feelings about the writing to Marjorie's dilemma:

> I think that maybe I am still afraid that even in the journal writing, I have to be able to see it all before I can say anything, or that, somehow, there has to be a right answer there. And so often, I just can't see everything.

Even as each of us interrupted the other to assure Katherine of our frequent inabilities to see "even small bits," as Cheryl said, Kevin brought up his initial fears of writing, and connected them to Katherine's uncertainties about the function of journal writing as well as the structures within which she worked that constantly encouraged the "right" answer:

> I really never wanted anyone to read what I wrote. And I'm not sure how much of that had to do with my fears about lack of ability as much as what I really might reveal. I wonder how much this aspect of our work together

might intimidate others who would like to do what we are doing? It's just always easier not to stir the waters, to just let things go by in the same old ways.

Beth, who had been listening intently, replied quietly to Kevin's query about intimidation:

You know, I worry that I can never see myself doing this with others, especially now that I'm an evaluator. It's not just that I'm in a different position now, but that teachers might see the research thing as a threatening construct. Or maybe administrators would see that as intimidating, if teachers did their own research, and that's what teachers would be reacting to when they pulled back.

I responded:

Beth, is this part of what you meant in your last writing about feeling separated from the group for a while, about pulling back? You were a teacher for almost twenty years, and now you are in a higher position in the scheme of things, yes? I mean, don't the teachers see you as above them now in the hierarchy? And so wouldn't that have some effect on their responses to you? Are you thinking that maybe what we are doing is just one more thing that will separate you from the everyday lives of teachers? Or that you have to pull back because the administrators with whom you are working won't like this? And yet what we're doing, I think, is trying to look at things that teachers or principals or counselors or superintendents can do every day in their classrooms or at faculty meetings or school board meetings, don't you think?

Beth paused for a bit, and we were silent as we waited for her to speak. It was clear to all of us that she was feeling uncertain, not only about her new job and its adjustments but also about her place within our collaborative work. She finally spoke, very quietly:

I *was* separating myself from this group for a while, but only in my head. I kept writing, I keep looking in this new job for places where I can work with some teachers in the ways that we are working. I keep coming to our meetings! [We all laughed, and yet it was apparent to us all that Beth was feeling some pain about these issues.] But, I guess what's been happening for a few weeks is that I'm feeling so unconnected to what I'm doing now because it's so new and to what I used to do for so many years, teaching, that I just feel adrift. And I'm afraid that I still need structure, that I need to feel in control in order to do a good job. And we don't have much structure here, or, and I know you'll laugh, any clear-cut answers. But it's almost something

> I had to go through, feeling separated, so I could see that we do have internal structure and a rhythm to what we are doing. In a way, it's my first emancipated feeling! I can let go here, and really try to look at things. The trick is to be able to feel this way, act this way, in my job. I guess I just worry that I can't make the same connections right away in my new situation, and that everyone sees it as such a right-answer kind of job.

Cheryl responded to Beth's dilemmas by noting her own teaching position as one in which everyone also expects correct answers. She talked about her own uncertain feelings about attempting to provide a variety of ways for her LD students to respond in class and yet, at the same time, attempting to teach the basic skills they needed:

> I have so much stress put on accountability and on basic skills of reading and math with my students, and yet I'm much more aware now, based on our work together and on my researching focus, that I, as well as other LD teachers, just don't give much leeway to students to respond in any ways that would encourage their thinking capabilities. Sometimes I wonder if it's better not to raise all these questions, because then we are really taking on huge problems and trying to change a lot of things! But it's like you said, Marjorie, once we've started this, it's hard to ignore all the things that pop up in our daily lives that we know need to be changed. I'm just not in a system that wants much change, but that doesn't mean that I'm not trying to modify my teaching. And I keep talking with the other teachers, even though we won't get any support for the kinds of things that we are looking at. But it's really hard. So Beth, maybe some of your withdrawal is because a lot of people would see the work of evaluator as a change-agent kind of thing? And so that's why you want to retreat to structure and definite answers?

Cheryl had raised some difficult questions for us all, and we talked at length about change. We discussed the changes that we all felt about ourselves as a result of our work together thus far, and acknowledged the ambiguities that characterized our attempts to "find out what's really going on." As Beth cracked, "most of the time, we don't want to know!"

We talked about Fullan's point (1982) that all real change involves loss, anxiety, and struggle. We were attempting not only to challenge but also to change our perceptions of the possibilities for ourselves, for our students, and for our colleagues as active agents in the world. We also were fighting to accept our uncertain reactions as a necessary part of our process. This struggle was, and continues to be, especially difficult, given the overlapping layers of assumptions and expectations through which we habitually view our roles, and the losses that we fear if we give up conceptions of ourselves as "in charge" and "in control."

Cheryl's comments moved us into a discussion of the many roles in education that presumed a position of authority and control. We talked about the predominant notion of change-agent as the one in charge of mandating and orchestrating change, and about how often this top-down conceptualization especially characterized administrative roles, such as Beth's position as evaluator or Marjorie's as state-appointed mentor. Cheryl was pushing Beth, in this conversation, to look at her role in somewhat different ways than that of determiner of others' changes. She was asking Beth to consider her role as evaluator as one in which she did not have to know all of the answers. But, as Cheryl said, "it's really hard" to do this, to let go of the need to control.

Just as we were beginning to push one another a bit to look and look again at assumptions and sources of uncertain reactions to our work, we also were able to laugh. We just could not seem to stay in the tension of an uncertainty for too long without looking for spaces where we could break the intensity of our discussions. We were, in a sense, realizing that we might be pushing ourselves into expectations of immediate and correct answers to the difficult issues with which we all were grappling. Our laughter dissolved this ironic possibility. As Beth was groaning about the long-term effort that she saw ahead of her in confronting her own and others' expectations for her work in this new job, I replied, "Well, didn't you know when you accepted my invitation that this was a lifetime commitment? Don't you remember signing those little emancipatory researcher membership forms?" Amidst the giggles and groans, Kevin remembered:

> I had a professor in my psychology program who was a Freudian, and when people would ask him in class for some kind of time-line for the course work, he always answered, "Well, we're going to have to think in terms of years."

"Oh, my gosh," Beth said, as we roared. "Did you think this would be years when you issued the invitation?"

I obviously had shared some of my own doubts about our collaborative processes as our work was unfolding, especially as they related to fears of imposition, to hesitancies about the appropriate

81

form and direction for our work, and to my role within the group. But here, as we laughed together, the group members pushed me to remember what had motivated me to really move beyond my own uncertainties and to finally invite this group of people to join with me in exploration. Beth said:

> Are you sure you don't know what you're doing? Are you sure that you don't have some big plan in your head about all this, and that you know when and how we'll be done with all this?

We laughed some more as I retorted:

> I think that we all would have a hard time saying that we didn't know what we were doing! But trust me. I do not have a big plan in my head about all of this! And you know how much I struggle with the whole idea that I'm supposed to know the answers because I'm the professor, just like you struggle because you're the teacher or the evaluator. I know what I'm doing on some level, I guess. I had formative ideas about all of this, you know that. But I truly don't even remember formally conceptualizing our collaboration before that infamous picnic.
>
> I mean, I had started this stuff with teacher-as-researcher a while back, because it's such a part of the writing process movement, and I could see its importance with my writing in-service work with teachers. I guess I had considered trying to explore the more emancipatory aspects of this with some of the teachers in my in-service work. I just didn't want to do only the writing research focus, I wanted it to be broader.
>
> I wanted to see how thinking of research in new ways could open up possibilities for teachers. Not that we would come up with new methods per se, but we would be looking at the ultimate reasons for doing research. One research question will lead into another, and maybe that will allow us to ask the harder questions about what we are doing and why.
>
> I want to argue that if enough teachers have faith in their own voices and know that they can examine the underlying sources of their own beliefs about teaching and research, then they can confront the power and control issues that are just everywhere in education, and that make us all feel like we have to have the right answers all the time, to prove that we're good teachers to somebody above us or to justify our positions to our students and maybe ourselves. So if this can help us gain a sense of ourselves and begin to explore and to generate our own knowledge bases about our teaching and research, then it might help us not sink back into the mud.
>
> And yet I know that I sink back all the time. Every time you ask me if I have a plan for this, part of me thinks, oh, I *should* know this, I *should* have a grand scheme for all that we are doing. And yet I'm fighting myself here to say that it's O.K. not to know exactly, that that's what we're about, to

participate in knowledge creation. Easy to say, incredibly hard to do gracefully! I feel all the time the push and pull of this, that it's just easier to sink, or to pull the covers up, as Cheryl says, than to fight.

And so how long will this take? Kevin's professor says it, we're talking in terms of life-work here, I'm afraid. I so wish, for me too, that I could say "we're done!"

"Well," said Beth, "I think that we're done for tonight anyway! Does that help?"

The constraints that we have conceptualized in thematic form and variation continue to bombard us. Beth has started to relax about the possibilities of our explorations being turned into packaged "empowerment kits." This clearly is not a "one-shot deal," guaranteed to produce emancipated educators in three easy steps. As she left our meeting that March night, Beth still was laughing about our exchanges, and yet her final comments point to the difficulties presented by these constraints of time, of multiple layers, of uncertain reactions:

> This is so tough. I guess that my dream of a smooth and easy transformation into an empowered educator is just that—a dream. This is real. And it's hard work. But I have to keep going. It's like Marjorie said, we just can't ignore or deny now. Oh boy!

As we agreed to keep going, these intertwined themes emerged in more intense variations than we had come to expect. As we moved into our second year together, the constraints with which we were grappling erupted in points of dissonance that challenged us to examine the very forms and intentions of our collaboration.

CHAPTER FOUR

Points of Dissonance

Points of dissonance are pinpricks in our consciousness; they sometimes sting at inopportune moments when we are most concerned with maintaining a smooth and unruffled countenance. We become adept at brushing away the annoyance, shooing the discrepancy from our line of vision, as we wave away a fly that has hovered too close to the edges of our personal space. Only when the buzzing becomes too persistent, when the sting finally penetrates beneath surface awareness, are we forced to directly confront the sources of dissonance that disrupt our equilibrium, our sense of balance in the world.

Within our group, we no longer were able to brush away or ignore the discrepancies that we had identified within our individual situations, in part because we had come to know one another and to care about the difficulties that each of us faced in our work together. By revealing ourselves and our individual struggles, we also had forged an interactive and supportive framework for our pursuits. Our sharing of individual perspectives and discrepancies and our caring about one another's struggles and concerns thus encouraged us to look, to probe, to stretch ourselves and one another within the context of our explorations. As Marjorie had stated, we could no longer deny the initially unnamed issues that had prompted our willingness to explore and to attempt to become challengers. The growing connections among our group members provided the support and the strength, as Cheryl had noted, for each of us to continue the work that we had begun.

However, we also had come to respect the distance that sometimes separated the spaces in which each of us struggled. As we moved into our second year of collaboration, it was clear that we all worked in different ways to identify the sources of the discrepancies we each felt. We also had differing conceptions of possible courses of action beyond the safety and comfort of our group, for challenging our assumptions and taken-for-granted educational roles and relationships. The discrepancies and our approaches to our work were different for each of us, and in our collaborations, we were beginning to see that we could not assume identical responses to our varied concerns.

Thus we were becoming aware of the balance that our collaborative efforts required as well as of the tensions that these sometimes created. We were trying to create equitable and consensual approaches to our research and dialogue. However, we were beginning to feel the tensions generated by the changing nature of our relationships in our syncopated movement through our explorations. We were discovering similarities *and* differences in our collective and individual concerns and possible courses of action. We were beginning to entertain the possibility that collaboration did not necessarily mean that we reached consensus on the issues, on the approaches, or even on the goals of our researching attempts.

Our struggles to maintain our equilibrium while tackling the constraints of time, of multiple layers of assumptions and expectations, and of uncertain reactions to the tensions generated by our pursuits exemplify the difficulties in acknowledging and maintaining these necessary balancing points. Martin and Mohanty (1986), in their discussion of the search for identity as a "rewriting of the self in relation to shifting interpersonal and political contexts," point to the tensions that are embedded in such balancing attempts:

> There is an irreconcilable tension between the search for a secure place from which to speak, within which to act, and the awareness of the price at which secure places are bought, the awareness of the exclusions, the denials, the blindness on which they are predicated. . . . The assumption of, or desire for, another safe place like "home" is challenged by the realization that "unity"—interpersonal as well as political—is itself necessarily fragmentary,

itself that which is struggled for, chosen, and hence unstable by definition; it is not based on "sameness," and there is no perfect fit. But there is agency as opposed to passivity. (206–208)

In our first year of meetings, we had forged "a secure place from which to speak." As we continued our collaboration, however, we were becoming aware that there were exclusions and areas of blindness for each of us within our secure and supportive meetings and dialogues. In our longing for a stability and a unity that we did not find in our individual educational contexts, we often could ignore, for a while, the dissonance stinging our unexamined expectations for "sameness" within our collaborative efforts.

At the same time, through our awareness of one another's situations, we also were able to begin asking questions of one another from the variety of our positions and perspectives. Those questions signaled at least our willingness to address the ways in which our perspectives differed as well as converged. In this way, we were beginning to search for the difficult balancing points of our individual and collective concerns. We also were beginning to see "that the questions that are asked—and, even more significantly, those that are not asked—are at least as determinative of the adequacy of our total picture as are any answers that we can discover" (Harding 1987, 7).

One particular episode within our group exemplifies the ways in which collaborative approaches, if not framed as continuous and yet constantly changing relationships, might lead to expectations of "sameness." However, the same episode illustrates ways in which collaborative associations also might work to challenge the blindness and passivity that can accompany static notions of unity as well as to raise heretofore unasked questions.

The Carton of Knowledge

Marjorie lugged the contact-paper-covered file carton from the trunk of her car and shoved it onto the front seat beside me.

"Look at this," she implored. "How am I ever going to cover all the material in these files?"

I started to sift through the manila file folders contained in the carton; each file had been carefully labeled by the department chairperson who usually taught this foundations of education course to undergraduates. Marjorie had been assigned to teach this course in her first semester of college teaching.

On this September 1987 afternoon, we were meeting to discuss her transition from high school to college teaching and from graduate student back to teacher. Marjorie described herself as "just beginning to recover" from the intensity of completing her doctoral degree as she now confronted the changes and demands of this new position. At first, I attributed her high-pitched inquiry to these stresses. My assessment was incomplete, of course, although I had not intended to trivialize or dismiss the strains of Marjorie's adjustments.

"Why do you think the department chairperson gave you her carton?" I queried.

"I'm sure that she's just trying to be helpful to me, to cut down on my preparation time, because she knows that I also have to spend much of my time supervising student teachers."

Marjorie started to pull some of the file folders from the carton, and as we began to sort through the materials in them, I started to feel some anger toward this chairperson. These files were her codification of the knowledge necessary for elementary education undergraduates; they were not Marjorie's in any sense.

The file on "historical perspectives" became a catalyst for points of dissonance to surface within each of us. As I pulled this file from the carton, a picture postcard of Michelangelo's "David" fell onto the car seat. Marjorie grabbed it and, trying to read the handwriting on the back of the card, began to create connections that she might make between "David" and the history chapter in her foundations textbook. What immediately began to emerge were Marjorie's remembrances of her viewing of the "David" and the feelings and events that surrounded that experience. It was her story of the "David" and its meanings for her that emerged, not the story her chairperson would have told around the figure of "David."

"Of course," Marjorie said quietly, as she paused in her narration. "How could I forget so quickly? It's what we have been trying to do in our teacher-researcher group all year, making our own connections and posing our own questions. How could I lose it so quickly? And what was I going to do to my students? Did I think that I was going to make the connections for them, tell their stories for them?"

I wondered about my anger in response to this file carton and all that it represented. As I wrote about this episode in my journal and thought about my written and spoken dialogues with Marjorie, I knew that some points of dissonance in myself were similar to those that Marjorie expressed to me. The file carton was a concrete manifestation of pressures that I continued to feel in my teaching, even as we had attempted, for over a year now, to look for ways in which we might consider ourselves as not just knowledge disseminators but knowledge creators. As much as I continued to try to develop classroom contexts and processes in which students could create their own connections among the themes, issues, and texts that we were exploring, I still worried. I worried, just as Marjorie had worried in her in-service workshops and as Cheryl had worried with her LD students, about covering the "material" of the course, about providing ample time and contexts for students to think, and about providing enough background and sources for students to begin their own searches for connections among the materials and content of the course and their lives. At the same time, I worried about imposing my own connections upon their situations, thus telling their own stories for them.

I listened to Marjorie struggle with the implications for her teaching of this file carton. As I listened, I continued to focus my attention on what I saw as the chairperson's imposition and on my admitted frustrations with Marjorie's initial responses.

As I later wrote in my journal, I realized that my anger at this chairperson represented my assumption that she was imposing her conceptions of the foundations course upon Marjorie. My anger also perhaps represented, to some extent, the recurrent fears that I might, in fact, be doing the same to my students, and now to the members of our collaborative group. Here again appeared my struggles with what I felt were discrepancies between my intentions as a teacher and co-learner and the institutionalized expectations for my role as teacher-authority. This felt discrepancy, with which I had been grappling openly in our collaborative group, now reemerged as a biting sting. I had to confront, yet again, these familiar feelings of confusion about this constant issue as well as to puzzle over my new anger. I realized that I had to look and look again at this discrepancy that I thought I already had addressed, and to admit that my assumptions underlying the tensions I felt about authority and imposition were multi-layered. As I reflected on the reemergence of these layers of assumptions, I also realized that I had to look at the extent to which my responses to this carton of knowledge and my interpretations of the chairperson's intent were based on my own conflicts rather than on any concrete evidence of the chairperson's attempts to manipulate or to control Marjorie's teaching.

Why was I angry even at Marjorie? I did express some frustration to her, even as she pulled this carton from her car trunk. Why couldn't she immediately see the contradictions encased in this carton? Why must she feel that she had to teach the course from the chairperson's perspective? What about our year's work in attempting to understand the meanings and forms and possibilities of emancipatory pedagogy and research? Didn't those possibilities begin with our understandings of ourselves as knowers in the world?

These questions are embarrassing in retrospect, for, as we started to talk about the carton, I began to realize that, although I was not toting a contact-paper-covered file carton of materials, I now might be lugging around, in my mind, layers of assumptions about appropriate "emancipatory" forms of knowledge creation through teaching and research. As I was able to see the possible compartmentalizing in my thinking and the ironic resulting imposition of my own assumptions on others, I finally began to view this file carton from another angle. I could now see this container as filled with files of underlying assumptions, not only for Marjorie but also for myself.

Stored Files

Once I could let the full sting of the file carton episode penetrate, I was able to look too at my responses to this situation from a "jolted" perspective. I think that some of the frustrations and confusions that the file carton raised within me had to do more with the very constraints and institutional impositions that I felt and to which I thought I often succumbed in my role as university professor than with Marjorie's responses per se. As much as I was committed to exploring the relational nature of teaching and research, I also was grappling with the contradictions that such perspectives raised for me as I worked within the university setting. Those contradictions had to do with the conception that contrasts classroom teachers' and university professors' work as practice versus theory. They also had to do with the separation of the roles of teacher and of researcher to which Schön (1983; 1987) and others[1] had pointed in highlighting the constraints of attempting critical and reflexive inquiry within hierarchical and bureaucratic schooling structures.

However, I believe that my frustrations also reflected my investment in our teacher-researcher group. I had invested myself, not only in exploring our own possibilities within alternative forms of research but also in emotional commitment and involvement in the group's collective endeavors. My responses to that carton of knowledge revealed for me another deeply embedded assumption that I thought I had eliminated earlier in our collaborative processes. However, this assumption reappeared as I had to look again at my frustrated and angry responses to the carton of knowledge. As much as I wanted to deny this assumption, I had to admit now that I somehow did take for granted that we all would proceed throughout our investigations in similar rhythms and directions. This assumption pointed to a concomitant emotional expectation on my part that the collective would provide constant shelter from institutional isolation. Another layer included the assumption that we all would define and act upon emancipatory possibilities in our lives in similar ways.

Yet the seductive aspects of "unity" were threatening to obscure the positive and necessary differences among our group. In my desire for the comforts of unity, I was ignoring the overlapping yet varying experiences that marked each of our understandings of our teacher-researcher work. I was as contained within these assumptions as was the chairperson with her carton of filed knowledge or Marjorie within her responses to perceived encapsulation.

The file carton prompted me to go back to my original hunches about the idea of teacher-as-researcher in this work. I knew now that I had to press beyond the descriptions and analyses I thus far had shared with our collaborative group about the origins of our present research endeavors, in order to confront the sources of my sense of dissonance.

I returned to the journal entries that chronicled, up to that point, my four years of in-service writing work with classroom teachers in one school district. During those four years, I had been conducting in-service programs for teachers on how to incorporate writing into their classroom work as a way for students to learn. As I worked with these teachers, who represented all subject areas and grade levels, kindergarten through 12th grade, I began to pose the concepts of writing as a way of learning and of discovery, and as a means by which the teachers could explore the empowering aspects of writing for themselves as well as for their students.[2]

What struck me as I reread my journal entries was the extent to which I grappled with the initial resistance of the teachers. Their resistance emerged in the in-service settings, I thought, not only because many of them had never experienced writing in these ways, but also because they could not envision a teaching-learning context in which such possibilities might flourish. The teachers constantly spoke of mandated curriculum requirements, administrative pressure for raised student achievement scores, and the restrictions of time and lack of student interest as impediments to the implementation of writing in their classrooms. Only when we began to write in our in-service context were some able to talk about ways in which their own writing enabled them to see themselves as learner-discoverers. However, at this point in my in-service work, I still was not examining the deeper sources of their resistance to these approaches to the teaching of writing. I just was pleased to see them willing to engage in the writing process with their students. If they no longer saw themselves as just dispensers of someone else's knowledge, and if they could experience with their students the possibilities of writing as a way of knowing and discovering, I felt some measure of success.

These in-service experiences clearly framed my thinking about the separation of educators' public and private worlds. As I continued my in-service work with the same group of teachers, I began to assume that we, as teachers, have to make personal meanings of emancipation before more public expressions and actions are possible. I began to assume this because I was faced with so many teachers who resisted considering that it might be possible to act as knowledge creators beyond the confines of their individual classrooms.

At the same time, the teachers continued to speak of the ways in which the writing in-service experiences began to inform both their students' and their own conceptions of themselves as knowers. I heard these testimonies as small personal expressions of teachers who felt that they were beginning, through the sharing of writing processes, to interact with their students in ways that affirmed them all as "knowers," at least within the confines of the classrooms. I assumed that these expressions of self as learner and creator were the necessary first steps before we could expand our actions into the institutional and social contexts that framed our work.

Ironically, I failed to see that the classrooms that were the sites of these teachers' inquiries into their own practice and their interactions with students also contained the very intersections of public and private worlds that I was seeking to address. There was no larger world in which to battle and to strive for equitable and reciprocal relationships; the classroom itself and the daily relationships among teachers, students, parents, counselors, and administrators provided the very "spaces where dialogue can take place and freedom can appear."

In confronting the stings I felt from the carton of knowledge episode, I now could see that I brought those separations of the public and private worlds into my work with the collaborative research group. I did not see that my own struggles with the issue of imposition within my own classrooms, within my in-service work, and within our group emanated from this continuing separation between my own ways of knowing and being in the world, and the supposedly large, visible, and authoritative ways of addressing issues of empowerment and emancipation in teaching and research. My small daily attempts to combat the distancing effects of the "authoritative voice" on the ways in which I wanted to enact my role as university professor, as in-service provider, or as researcher did not yet count, in my mind, as examples of "political" acts that could interrupt taken-for-granted and oppressive situations. Nor had I understood as an example of such action the attempts of the in-service teachers to share with their students and with one another their developing perceptions that writing is a way of knowing.

In reflecting on these assumptions that had developed in my in-service work with teachers, I also returned to the frameworks that supported my attempts to teach writing as process, as a way of knowing and discovering. I reviewed the work of writing researchers and scholars who had influenced my approaches to the teaching of writing and to the formation of interactive in-service contexts. In that reviewing process, I knew that I had not missed the connections in their work that pointed to the reciprocal nature of teaching and learning, writing and thinking, responding and revising. What I had missed, however, were the implications in their work that constant interplay occurs between one's public and private worlds as one participates in these processes.

Thus, both Moffett (1968; 1981; 1988) and Britton (1970; 1987), in their conceptualizations of writing as process and as centered within individuals' personal observations and responses, pointed to the intertwined relationships among experience, thought, language, and culture.[3]

Ann Berthoff (1981; 1982) argues that reading and writing happen in social, political, and psychological contexts. She calls attention to the possibilities of teaching composition as a dialectical process in which students can rediscover the power of language to generate meanings.

Shirley Brice Heath's ethnographies (1983; 1987) examine the influence of culture upon children's language development and the importance of "audience community" (Heath and Branscombe, 1985) in that development. As well, Karen LeFevre (1987) contends that much of the writing process approach and of contemporary composition theory incorrectly views rhetorical invention as the private act of an individual writer for producing a particular text; she argues that rhetorical invention is better understood as a social act, in which an individual, who is at the same time a social being, interacts in a distinctive way with society and culture to create something. LeFevre recommends that the writing process be viewed as individuals' relationships to others through the social nature of language as well as through the social structures in which they live.

Knoblauch (1988) argues that teachers and students must research the ways in which learning and knowing are expressed through language that not only reflects but also shapes the values, world assumptions, and images of self and others. Thus, writing as a "way of learning or knowing" does not stop with "personal connections" but "proceeds to a full awareness of the interpretive communities (themselves endlessly evolving) that shape those connections from the very beginning" (135).

Although these theorists pointed to conceptions of the inventing individual and the sociocultural context as co-existing and mutually defining, I continued to think sequentially. I continued to harbor the implicit assumption, as we began our collaborative explorations, that our personal explorations of the possible meanings and forms of emancipatory research and pedagogy must precede any collective or social enactments of those meanings. I was not acknowledging the ways in which personal experience is discursively produced and constantly open to redefinition (Weedon 1987).

As I reviewed these frameworks that influenced my initial in-service work, I began to see the narrow and separate ways in which I had defined personal and social/political perspectives. The "carton of knowledge" episode threw my deeply embedded assumption into relief against the very nature of our explorations. I realized that I had been maintaining the "chasm that separates what we know as our public and private worlds" (Grumet, 1988a, xv) even as I thought that I had been working toward ways of acknowledging their reciprocal and intertwined relationships.

My reflections enabled me to recognize the linear, sequential manner in which I had been viewing the theoretical foundations of my writing in-service work. I did not fully realize that the biographical and the social constantly intersect. Thus, my expectations for "appropriate" actions which framed my responses to, and interpretations of, "the carton" were based on my linear manner of thinking. As I placed my reflections within the context of our collaboration, I also began to more fully understand why feminist scholars have maintained, even in the face of media trivialization and misinterpretation, that "the personal is political." The phrase, I realized, embodies the same tension to which Martin and Mohanty (1986) refer in attempting to find a safe place from which to speak and act, while at the same time attempting to be aware of the exclusions that the boundaries of such places create. That tension does not allow for the collapse of the phrase into a simple equation, for the tension arises from the constantly shifting boundaries of particular historical and biographical conditions. Thus the statement "the personal is political" is a way of understanding oneself in relation to shifting interpersonal and political contexts, and thus as multiple and sometimes even self-contradictory (deLauretis 1986). It also is a way of acknowledging the possibilities for individuals to create a more humane and just world, given awareness of their capacities to see and to confront the exclusions and denials, even as they live and work within the boundaries of institutions or situations that do not encourage such awareness and action.

In my developing understanding of that phrase, "the personal is the political," I also could see why those who want to enact research as an interactive, negotiated, and reciprocal process between the researched and the researchers draw from feminist approaches. In acknowledging the varying perspectives and contexts of individuals, feminist analyses draw on women's experiences to provide new resources for research, to center the purposes of research on and for women, and to locate the researcher in the same critical plane as the overt subject matter—that is, the race, class, and gender assumptions, beliefs, and behaviors of the researchers themselves are placed within the frame of the picture that they attempt to paint (Harding 1987). This acknowledgement of the varying perspectives and contexts of individuals could inform any research that attempts to be a democratized process of inquiry, and that recognizes the necessities, and yet concurrent difficulties, of participants' voicing their different experiences of the same processes and events (Brodkey 1987).

I think that I had approached our collaborative work with these concepts as a framework, and yet, until the "carton of knowledge" episode, I had not fully understood their implications for our work. Given the sting that the carton had provided, I had to return to my original assumptions in order to pull apart the layers of my experience that had reinforced linear conceptions of one's emergence from private into public realms of discourse and action. My linear vision, replicating the separation of theory and practice, thought and action, personal and public that permeates traditional educational processes and contexts, had obscured my understandings of the possibilities of their interactive and changing relationships. Only the long-term and changing nature of the interactions within our research group had allowed my assumptions to continue to surface as points of dissonance, and thus had created the space in which I could examine the sources of my contradictory assumptions. Within the constant interplay between the individual and collective meanings that emerged in our collaborative efforts, I finally was able to challenge my own linear and compartmentalized views of our work and to begin to view our collaborative processes as the interactive and constantly changing relationships that I had originally claimed them to be.

Setting Aside the Carton

As Marjorie and I spoke and wrote to one another about the "carton of knowledge" and its ramifications for us as individuals as well as collaborative group members, we agreed that we both were

96

shocked, to some degree, by our responses to that carton. We both expressed some resignation and dismay that we had to confront, again, the same layers of assumptions that we thought we had excised in earlier discussions and writing within our group.

However, we also were both able to laugh, finally, at the constant reemergence of another assumption: we agreed that we still were presuming, somehow, that if we had attempted to address the stings, the pain would then cease. Marjorie referred to this reemergent layer in our October 4, 1987, meeting, as we discussed with the group the stings that had signaled our points of dissonance:

> I guess that, just because we can point out our own dissonance, it doesn't mean that we're done. Oh no, here's that theme again! [We laughed, as Marjorie groaned.] Maybe, because we are trying to see ourselves as people who can take action in our worlds, we also have to see that we aren't going to change everything around us. This is like a never-ending battle. Maybe you don't resolve points of dissonance—in yourself or in situations. Maybe what you do is move beyond them, or at least around them. And maybe part of that movement is just in how you begin to look [at things] differently.

The difficulties encased within the carton of knowledge, then, had to do not only with our resurfacing layers of assumptions but also with the difficulties in knowing how "to look differently" at these points of dissonance so that their stings, while still painful, would not incapacitate us. To look differently, to look again and again, to look simultaneously for the safe place as well as for the exclusions—all of these efforts required us to change to see situations from a different vantage point. Our moves were slow and often filled with frustrations and pain.

Marjorie continued to wrestle with the implications of the carton of knowledge as she settled into her routine at the college. She began to view the carton as a symbol of her continuing struggle with her layers of assumptions about the issues of prescription and about compliance with others' expectations in her role as teacher. In our discussions of the episode, she began to attribute part of her shock and compliant reaction to the chairperson's carton as almost a throwback to her habitual responses to persons in authority within a school setting.

Further, she began to make connections between these habitual responses and her confusion about the seemingly contradictory aspects of content and process both in her in-service work and in her years of science teaching. She had been working, in our explorations, to see these contradictions as part of a continuum and not as an either-or proposition in teaching. As part of her researching efforts, she had focused on her prescriptive assumptions about "good teaching" as an opportunity to examine the sources of her underlying assumptions and expectations for herself as a teacher who is "in control" and who is anxious to "do it right." Especially like Beth, who struggled with similar assumptions, Marjorie had confronted these issues in various contexts of her work throughout our collaborative investigations. She found her reactions to the carton of knowledge, as I found mine, to be painful examples of the entrenched nature of these very layers of assumptions and expectations for herself that she had been researching.

In a journal entry of October 25, 1987, Marjorie wrote of her beginning attempts to figure out some ways of "moving around" or "looking differently" at the sources of these converging points of dissonance:

> After being so strongly committed to teacher-as-researcher for over a year, I was shocked myself to see how shook up I felt when removed from an environment at graduate school where everyone wanted to hear my thoughts. And I have become so used to the sharing and support of our research group. Unchallenged by any real live teaching situation, other than my inservice workshops, it was easy to have confidence. I think the challenge for me now has to do with admitting that I have wanted, for years, to be seen by others as "doing it right." And maybe, in the supportive context of the group, I was beginning to think that I was doing this right and therefore that I would be done with these issues. Even though I could see how I used to think that there was a "right way" to teach science, and even though I think that I have moved from that position, maybe I was just moving that assumption into our work.
>
> I believe that philosophically I now have much to bring to this new job, but I now also see that I still wanted to do what was expected of me . . . and it's hard to know that when you're new. I knew, I guess, after a while, what was expected of me in our group. But that feeling came through all of our discussion and writing back and forth. And even now, it does keep changing. There is very little opportunity to talk to anyone at school, and what was there for me seemed to come in the form of the "cartons." What I really wanted was an opportunity to explore the cartons with someone, to benefit from the experience of others who had been around for a while. It felt like the cardboard cartons were negating me, though, putting me out of the picture altogether.

Although Marjorie had taught high school biology for twelve years, and had taught elementary school for five years before that, this was her first venture into college-level teaching. Furthermore, she was the only one of the five graduate students in our teacher-researcher group who had completed her doctoral studies as a full-time student. The other members of the group were working full-time in their teaching or administrative positions as they pursued their graduate studies and as they participated in our collaborative efforts. Although she had worked extensively as a mentor in providing the science workshops for elementary school teachers as she completed her graduate work, Marjorie also had enjoyed the aspects of community that often accompany full-time graduate study.

Marjorie admitted that she was surprised at the unexpected isolation that she experienced as she entered the new context of college-level teaching. She had expected that there would be much more time and space in which to discuss issues with other faculty members than she had experienced in her public school teaching. She noted, in our October 4, 1987, meeting, that her participation in our collaborative group had heightened not only her expectations but also her desires for dialogue and interaction as ways of challenging old assumptions. Thus, in looking for an opportunity to "explore the cartons" with a colleague, Marjorie was trying to look differently at an old, and by now familiar and examined, assumption: she should do what was expected of her by the chairperson, without questioning and without discussing the implications of that carton for her work. She was trying, in her search for collegial discussion about the carton, not to let that container, with its folders of others' conceptualizations of her work, negate her.

Marjorie captured, in a journal entry of October 29, 1987, not only her sense of isolation in her new job but also the difficulties inherent in her attempts to act, within other contexts, upon the understandings that she thus far had developed about the sources and nature of her layers of assumptions:

> I had to fight my fears that I couldn't face all of this alone. I missed my two and a half years of support from the university community in analyzing all that this carton represented. I wanted our teacher-researcher group there with me to discuss all the layers in the box. I really feel right now that without the collaborative experience, there's a dimension of personal liberation that you don't touch. Having experienced the community, I feel a

challenge to go back and find it at a more personal level. That's exactly where I am. I almost have a fear that this doesn't exist apart from the group. Our collaboration has opened me up inside. It's a kind of freedom. It allows a response from you that has never been, that's never had a place to express itself.

Marjorie, in speaking of her wish to go back to the personal to explore the dimensions of liberation that she had thus far experienced in our collaboration, expressed the fluid and reciprocal movement between the spaces of public and personal worlds that I previously had only understood as linear and sequential. At the same time, Marjorie acknowledged that her fears that "this doesn't exist apart from the group" were grounded in the immediate difficulties of transposing her present understandings of her assumptions, as well as our collaborative processes, into contexts that replicated the very preunderstandings that she was working to excavate and to change. The seductive and selective aspects of "unity" about which Martin and Mohanty (1986) had warned, and with which I had been wrangling, were difficult for her to resist as well, for we had found comfort and a sense of security within our collaborative spaces.

However, we were making efforts to see beyond the boundaries of our collaboration in order to bring into view what we were excluding as well as including in our explorations. Because of these attempts to "look differently," I do think that Marjorie and I were able to confront these familiar yet disconcerting layers of assumptions in our thinking with a swiftness that ordinarily might not have characterized our encounter with the file carton. We clearly were not finished with our excavations, but our reflective writing and discussions about our points of dissonance made us acutely aware of their stings. In fact, we agreed that our interactions may have allowed us to acknowledge that which we ordinarily might have ignored or suppressed or dismissed. At this point, we regarded awareness and willingness to reveal our points of dissonance among ourselves as well as within our educational settings as protection against the dangers inherent in unexamined notions of "unity" and "sameness."

In a sense, we were becoming sensitive to what C. A. Bowers (1987) calls the power of the "natural attitude" and to what Martin and Mohanty (1986) refer to as the tendency of the dangerously narrow, self-enclosing definition of "unity" to conceal the very areas of shared culture that need to be named and thus illuminated and examined. In arguing that community and tradition can serve as sources as well as impediments to empowerment, Bowers (1987) notes:

> An understanding of embeddedness, of continuities, and of cultural and community membership seems essential to the formal educational process carried on in the classroom, but this understanding needs to be balanced by an ability to make explicit (and thus politicize) aspects of taken-for-granted beliefs and practices that are injurious in both an individual and communal sense. (157)

Our points of dissonance are constant reminders of the difficulties of such pursuits. The points tend to sting as we move further from our group and into contexts that encourage and reward the individualistic and rationalistic modes of consciousness. As these stings become more biting and constant, we still tend to retreat into our group not only for support to continue our explorations but also for the validation that our pursuits are worth the pain that each of us feels in the disjuncture between the collective and the individual contexts.

We all feel that we want to be able to act as "knowers" in our educational settings; none of us feels that we can recover our own possibilities only within the confines of our group, and further, none of us has the luxury of remaining within the group's comfortable boundaries. Each day we face contexts that do not support alternative perspectives. One goal of our collaborative efforts is to be able to act within these contexts as we do within our collective spaces, and to maintain a sense of balance as we move in and out of these constantly changing situations. In a sense, these balancing points consist of constant efforts to not fall back into the open carton, which could enclose and protect us from the stings that we would prefer to avoid.

Marjorie captures this dilemma in her journal:

> It still bothers me. There are two cartons now and both are sitting on my desk in a very small and over-crowed study. I've told myself and even my friends that I'm just storing them. The truth, however, is that I have not been able to move them to a storage location. They are right on the desk top taking up space and I still choose to keep them there. I think about moving them every day but I haven't found a reason to yet. That's how it is . . . it feels like I have to be able to give myself a reason that would make it O.K. to move them a few feet away. I'm getting a little less compulsive about having to

check each folder before preparing a lesson myself, but there's still a fear that there might be something important that I'll leave out, or a better way to present something than what I've thought up. If I'm really pressed for time, I omit using them [the ideas from the box], and I do know that the best classes have been the ones that were mine alone. I shock myself again and again that the cartons are still on my desk top.

After she wrote this in her journal, Marjorie moved one of the cartons into her storage room upstairs. We agreed that letting go of our fears and expectations about the "shoulds" of our work and our whole lives comes in small and sometimes barely discernible acts. We had come to understand that taking action beyond the supportive boundaries of our group required conviction and courage. One carton remained in her study.

Balancing Points

As we continued to expand our understanding of the possibilities in conceiving of ourselves as teacher-researchers, and as we struggled with the forms that such conceptions of ourselves might take in various educational settings, we all agreed that confronting our stings of dissonance was a form of action in our daily lives. The confrontations themselves were an aspect of our constant attempts to draw connections between the present disjunctures of our public and private worlds.

We especially realized, after the "carton of knowledge" episode, that our assumptions and our conceptions of possibilities differed, depending upon our individual settings and situations. We also knew that acting apart from our collective was difficult, at best. We still flailed about in our attempts to let go of our assumptions that there existed "right" ways in which to implement our explorations; we all still were convinced, at one point of another, that we probably were not "doing it right." We all were fairly certain that, when we left our collaborative meetings, we were alone in our attempts to even understand what becoming challengers might mean for teachers and students. We at least could admit these assumptions to one another, and we bemoaned how easily we got stuck in the prescriptive paradigm that controlled the majority of our educational work and interactions.

The "file carton" episode thus has become a symbol for the difficulties inherent in our attempts, as well as for the possibilities of balance and evenness of movement between our individual contexts and the community of our researching efforts. However, the carton also signifies the various levels of encapsulation about which Harding (1987), deLauretis (1986), Martin and Mohanty (1986) warn. One can become entrapped within collaborative assumptions just as easily as within individual assumptions; thus, one aspect of our research began to include explorations of these balancing points between our personal and collective interactions.

We wondered about the extent to which such points are the same or different for each of us, and the influence of our collaborative approach upon our perceptions of those points. Can balancing points be points of dissonance in another form, depending upon individual or collaborative perspectives?

As we continued to discuss the carton of knowledge and our reactions to its multiple representations in our varying points of dissonance, we began to examine these questions in light of our developing notions of collaborative processes. At that point, we agreed that collaboration had encouraged our individual confrontations with our points of dissonance and had provided a place for us to ponder their stings and to give voice to our contradictions as well as our strengths. Yet our work together had not resulted in identical or simultaneous responses to points of dissonance or to the emergence of a collective voice. Rather, we continued to acknowledge the very difficult dance between the particular and the generalizable that characterized our explorations; we had become aware not only of the variety of meanings and possible forms of emancipatory pedagogy and research but also of the changing collective and individual interactions and perceptions that were inherent in our searches. However, the carton of knowledge, although revealing the very depths to which we ourselves had filed our assumptions and expectations, also encouraged us to persevere in our explorations. We had found at least one balancing point in our collaboration that allowed us to confront our points of dissonance as well as to begin definition of our own possibilities:

> Teachers must act in an imperfect world. We have no choice but to risk ourselves. The choice is to consider the risk private or to build a community that accepts vulnerability and shares risks. Vulnerability is endurable in a community of care and support—a community in which members take time telling and listening to the stories of each other's journey. . . . We need

people who listen to us and to whom we listen, who help in the narration of our story, so we can more readily recognize our changing values and meanings. . . . We must begin to scrutinize and become intentional about the communities within which we teach. We must seek out new coalitions and work intentionally at the social fabric that surrounds those of us who are called to be teachers. (Huebner 1987, 26–27)

We had chosen to become vulnerable and to share risks, and in so doing, we also had to acknowledge that our sense of balance in the world, as Beth noted laughingly, tended to fluctuate. But in this conscious choosing, we were beginning to feel "agency as opposed to passivity," even though that agency often was accompanied by stings. Those stings were more important for our individual and collective growth than were the particular points of dissonance because they impelled us to examine our assumptions about our work, again and again.

CHAPTER FIVE

Becoming Challengers

The "carton of knowledge" episode reverberated throughout our research group. The points of dissonance with which each of us was struggling emanated from similar intersections among our particular situations and the institutions and social constructs within which we lived and worked, even as they manifested themselves in individual contexts and even as we responded to them in unique ways.

As Marjorie and I told our stories of this episode, the group members reacted to the variations in our telling, noting our different emphases and responses to the carton as well as their own responses and interpretations of its significance.

Persistent Interruptions

At the same time, group members began making connections between our battles with the "carton of knowledge" and their own struggles with their unique versions of the same episode. The carton existed, in one form or another, in everyone's daily life as an educator. As we discussed our varying concrete examples of the prescriptions and controls that permeated our understandings and enactments of our roles as educators, we began to interrupt each other, no longer content to wait politely in turn. These persistent interruptions signified not only our ever-growing comfort and familiarity with each other but also that "sense of urgency" about which Katherine had spoken so early in our meetings.

The urgency now centered on our attempts to be aware of the balances that we were trying to maintain within our collaboration. As the carton so vividly exemplified, we could be as encased within our own perspectives as those neatly filed folders of knowledge. We at least were now aware of the possible exclusions and points of blindness that the boundaries of our collaboration might create, and yet, at the same time, we did not want to remain only at the borders of our explorations, afraid to take a stance and to pursue our own possibilities within the context of becoming challengers.

Thus, with the metaphoric opening and displacement of that carton of knowledge, we felt a heightened sense of urgency to be aware, to continue to "look further and bigger," as Kevin had said, to see beyond our borders as well as within them. We had begun to sense the concrete possibilities of placing ourselves at the center, as knowers and creators, of our teaching and researching endeavors. We now also were aware of the pain of possible occlusion of vision, of the omissions as well as the expansive visions, that might be inherent within that new stance. Marjorie noted:

> I don't think that anyone can understand what emancipatory action can be—individually or collectively—until you go through yourself to look at the sources of how you feel and act. Raising questions about the carton and about my reactions to it kept everything from sliding into neat categories. You're free to ask questions, not driven to answers, not pushed to closure.

Our work gained momentum as we excitedly interrupted each other, not allowing ourselves, as much as possible, to "slide into neat categories" of perspective or response.

Becoming Vocal

Katherine especially tried to call attention to the difficulties she experienced, which she felt other teachers experienced too, in trying to avoid those neat categories that the carton of knowledge represented. In the beginnings of our collaboration, she had attributed these difficulties to the hectic routine and often mandated curriculum of the elementary teacher within the self-contained classroom. As she often said in our meetings, "there's just no time to think during the day. And when I get home, I most often don't *want* to think about it all!"

As Marjorie and I discussed the carton of knowledge, however, Katherine was the first to draw the analogy between that carton and her own school. She began to look back at her original interest in Valerie and at her later movement away from that child as her research focus. As she talked about her gradual and mostly unconscious shift in research focus toward her relationships with the teachers and administrators in her school, Katherine now saw comparisons between her reactions and frustrations to those relationships and Marjorie's and my responses to the carton of knowledge. As she began to look again at her situation, Katherine also began to talk more in the group, and she also began to write; as she noted, the writing was "just a little bit again." Katherine's examinations of these issues had begun before the carton episode, but that metaphor allowed her to begin to look directly at possible reasons for her often encapsulated feelings within her collegial relationships. As she said, "you'd think that I'd feel more boxed-in with my first-graders in that classroom all day, but I don't. It's the one place in school where I feel most free."

Katherine's questions about the sources of her own feelings of frustration in the school and their connections to others' expectations and constructions of how she should be as a teacher had been gaining momentum, even before our encounters with the carton. In our meeting of April 6, 1987, she had asked:

> *Now* what can I do? How can I challenge this huge system that has us all having to bow to someone else's version of how we should be teachers? I feel as though it's the outside forces that stop the processes that we start here. What I've gained from this group has me frustrated right now. There is a lot happening in school, and now I just can't go home and say, that's it. Now I can't say that it doesn't involve me. What I've found out here is that I am somebody, that I do have something to say, but then at school, I get stuck. I don't know what to do to begin to raise some questions about what is going on there.

Marjorie responded:

> Maybe you are getting to the point where your frustrations will allow you to speak up there, to pose some questions?

Katherine answered:

I don't know. Now we're having teacher meetings with the principal on how we can make ourselves look good on state test scores. People are really upset at this total emphasis on test scores, and the principal is trying to cover all our bases.

Cheryl queried:

Is there something in the processes that we've been sharing that could help you there?

Katherine:

I don't know yet how the teachers in my school could have this same shared sense of action—collective action. I think that the teachers are willing to work at it, to try, and yet there is this tremendous feeling that we can't fix it!

Katherine was pushing us here, reminding us of the feelings of powerlessness that sometimes overwhelmed her once she left the secure place that our meetings had become and reentered her elementary school. She felt movement for herself within our group as she explored her own reactions and expectations in her teaching situation, but she did not feel that same sense of movement once she left our group. She raised this point of dissonance again and again, and the "carton of knowledge" just accentuated her growing questions and feelings of contradiction between the focus of her work within our collaboration and her situation in the elementary school.

Katherine's points of dissonance remain a central question in our work. We all agree that many teachers share this same sense of frustration with the larger systems that seem to control definitions of curriculum content and pedagogical effectiveness, and thus teachers' sense of themselves. To what extent can collaborative work like ours encourage teachers to look beyond the mandates of others? To what extent can this work encourage teachers to look to themselves and their relationships with other educators in order to challenge, individually and collectively, the frameworks and structures that perpetuate such feelings of powerlessness and frustration? What actions can teachers take to change these frameworks that appear impenetrable to those who are ensconced in classrooms and separated from one another by walls of imperatives and by systems of checks and controls?

We worked on what still seemed, in the scheme of things, to be very small suggestions for action. We were only coming to the understanding that our offices and classrooms *were* the major arenas in which we could work for equitable and reciprocal relationships. And so, in this April meeting, we still were forming our suggestions as examples of the "bit by bit" connections that we might effect between our collaborative undertakings and our daily work. We were trying to see these minute suggestions as representative of potential forms of action among groups of teachers who also wished to become challengers in worlds that more often rewarded the followers. These attempts to "look differently" continued to be difficult for us all.

I asked Katherine:

What chance is there of turning your teacher committee on test scores into a research group like this?

Marjorie responded, as Katherine hesitated:

The teachers I'm working with in the science workshops have so much anger. My workshop is ending up being a place to vent their anger. When I ask them to identify discrepancies, not just in the teaching of science but in their teaching situations, then, WHOMP, they respond with so much anger. Like Katherine, I'm not sure what to do with all of that.

Beth asked:

Is there any resistance to change too, though?

Marjorie:

Oh yes! And that's another difficult thing about what I think that we are trying to do here. Look at how long it's taken all of us to be willing to look beyond the standard response of, "Oh, that's just how it is."

I responded:

That's the scary part for me, because there is always an element of resonance for everyone in that standard response. The hugeness of the situation leads so many of us, at one time or another, to just shrug our shoulders and say,

"How can just a few of us change things?" Or, if we do press for change, if we can no longer stand the ways things are and we don't accept them as just inevitable, if we ourselves are willing to change, then the other scary response is, "What if we are left standing alone?"

Katherine finally spoke, after listening quietly to these various interruptions:

Maybe we keep going back to the structures as we know them because we don't know what else to do. Does emancipation always have to lead to frustration?

We continued to debate this major point of dissonance in the months leading up to the carton of knowledge episode. We also tried to take the "small, bit by bit steps" that could extend what we saw as the strengths of our collaboration into our individual educational settings. We all wanted to be able to do similar kinds of work within these institutional settings, and yet the difficulties inherent in such transpositions were becoming more and more apparent to us. Those very settings contained major manifestations of oppressive situations and relationships that appeared, in many times and circumstances, to be immutable.

At this point, we still were working to illuminate our individual understandings and experiences of those situations; these attempts, in and of themselves, required much effort, as we struggled with the barriers of time, of layers of assumptions, of our ambiguous reactions. Thus, we had not yet begun to focus on attempts to see clearly the concomitant possibilities contained within those same settings. We were afraid, we admitted to one another as we entered into our second year of explorations, that maybe, most of the time, the answer to Katherine's questions about the inevitability of frustration might be "yes."

We were, however, at a point in our work, during the spring and summer of our second year together, where we at least were able to acknowledge the difficulties that we were experiencing. Those difficulties especially centered around our ambiguous responses to our attempts to even identify as oppressive the many educational situations, and our responses to them, that we had come to take for granted. As Katherine kept asking, "Then what do I do? Is it enough for teachers to really want to be researchers, to see things in a new way? That's hard enough, as far as I can tell!"

We all were able to identify the ambiguous reactions that Katherine's questions elicited in us. How far could we or should we go in attempting to transpose the processes and intentions of our work together into our schools and offices and classrooms? Could the boundaries of our group be flexible and expansive enough to allow us the congruence in our public and private worlds to which we supposedly aspired? As we discussed these questions, we also talked about the ways in which seeing things in a new way did not guarantee clear perceptions or untainted visions. These difficult questions heightened our concerns about the potential reification of "new" ways of seeing into prescriptive mandates; further, I believe that they at least laid the foundations for my own confrontation, during the carton episode, with the ways in which I, in fact, was doing exactly what we had feared. Beth's constant query, "What's to prevent this process from being packaged and taken on the road?" had new meaning for me, especially during these early times of formative questions, and later at the time of our struggles with the "carton of knowledge."

As we met during the spring and summer of 1987, Katherine continued to raise her questions in a manner that, although always gentle and quiet, was more insistent and urgent than before. She said that it was not that she felt incapable of formulating her own responses to her problems with her school, but rather that she truly felt pressed up against institutional walls and could see no room for movement of any kind.

However, in sharing these frustrations with the group, Katherine also engaged us in the immediate situations of many classroom teachers who have the luxury of neither time nor space within which to debate and discuss the sources of dissonance that plague all educators' work. Hers was a concrete effort to carve out that necessary time and space with those teachers and administrators in her building as well as with us so that her frustrations with the system itself would not shut her down completely as a teacher. She did not want to drop out of teaching, but, at times, did consider dropping out of our collaborative group. The pain that erupted through her points of dissonance was intense, and she often felt that there was nothing that she could do to change the circumstances of her situation.

However, Katherine stayed with us, in part, as she said, because she was tired of blaming herself for the inadequacies that she felt as a teacher. These feelings propelled her into an examination of the metaphorical "cartons of knowledge" from which, for years, she had been drawing her expectations for herself as a teacher.

As she attempted to look again at her frustrations, Katherine's attention was drawn toward an examination of her reactions to what she saw as the rigid, heavy-handed style of those who worked in and administered her school. She focused upon particular problems within her building and upon her tendencies to internalize these problems as her fault, in part. As she did so, Katherine began to see how this internalization of the system's problems as her own had prevented her from examining the constructs and expectations that emerged from the intersections of school and societal structures as well as from her position within those structures.

As she focused on these intersections, Katherine began to interrupt our discussions with her newly defined "sense of urgency." She presented us with several dilemmas in her daily work, and asked us to consider with her the possibilities for her actively dealing with each of these.

The first dilemma concerned the student teachers with whom she was working as an adjunct reading instructor at a local university. In our meeting of July 30, 1987, she noted:

> You know, we talk a lot about the culturally embedded and controlling notions of appropriate teacher behavior, and about how our work together and being teacher-researchers could be emancipatory. But when I'm faced with these student teachers who only want to know prescriptions of how to do this test or how to handle this child, I get really scared. It's like I've been saying—I no longer can ignore how fixated on absolutes the teaching profession seems to be and how much that reflects the control issues in education. But at the same time, I'm a reading specialist who teaches first-graders and I want these student teachers to know how to diagnose kids with reading problems too.
>
> So part of me wants to tell them "what to do." You know, "Do this and you'll be effective." But part of me now wants to also encourage them to be researchers of their own ideas and of their own development as teachers and of the controlling aspects of teaching and society that could take over their lives. So what can I do? I can't just teach them all these prescriptions, and hand them checklists, and then finally say, "Well, what do you think and feel, and where do you think all of those assumptions have come from?" I can't just tack on at the end all this that we do together in our group.

Katherine's questions about working with her student teachers reflected, in part, the questions that Marjorie had raised about her work with the in-service teachers. They also reflected the dichotomies of theory–practice, process–content, reflection–action, private–public that permeate positivist orientations in education, and indeed our daily lives. Her questions especially alluded to the overwhelming difficulties of creating preservice and in-service programs that provide room for teachers to engage in interactive and reflexive considerations of their work and of the contexts that limit as well as help them in teaching.

We began to interrupt one another, however, as we pondered Katherine's dilemma with her student teachers. These interruptions were different from the quiet and measured responses that we had given to our earlier discussions. A sense of excitement and of movement permeated our meetings in this second year, and although we could not name our directions, we knew that we were now, as I said, "on a roll."

Cheryl responded to Katherine's situation by noting:

You know, there's no place else where I can come and think about my work and about all the other factors that we have been discussing that influence how we think about our work. Maybe if others, including student teachers who don't have much experience yet, could experience the kind of sharing and exploring that we do, then maybe it would trigger a desire, a demand that some time and space be provided for this.

Marjorie answered:

But you know that many teachers feel their hands are tied, that there's nothing that they can do. They feel such administrative constraints and the administrators feel such constraints from the state. It's a vicious circle and everyone blames everyone else. But I do think that there are already teachers out there who are doing it, doing what we do, and they just don't have official sanction.

Kevin responded:

Yes, I think that's true. I think that many of us have experienced at some time in our lives the feelings of connectedness that we have here. What's different about this is that it extends beyond a support group because we keep focused on our work and on uncovering our underlying assumptions that tend to keep us unaware of these larger issues. I really see this as a challenge, not a threat to teachers or administrators. We just have to keep posing this kind of work and these kinds of attitudes as a challenge.

Katherine:

So can you still teach content while posing challenges to people, to teachers and to students, to become more aware, to take action?

Beth:

Yes! We just have to keep showing how this isn't just an add-on feature to student teaching programs or in-service. It's so hard for teachers to not see everything as one more add-on because they already are expected to cover so much. If they could see that this was already a part of what they are doing every day—that it's just a way of looking at what you are doing so that you don't become a passive robot. The problem is that most teachers only ever are presented with "tinker-toy" models of teaching and we can't impose this work as one more add-on to the tinker-toy model.

I responded:

Yes. There's a tremendous difficulty here—how do we not present this as yet one more mandated part of a teacher's life and yet encourage people to look beyond the tinker-toy constructions that control much of what they think they have to do as teachers. It's another balancing point, huh?

Beth asked:

So, I still worry. Do you think that we could just turn into another form, an acceptable professional form of empowerment?

We all shrieked, as Beth continued:

Well, what I mean is that nothing would please some administrators I know more than to think that we were doing "research" in their terms. That's what scares me about the phrase "teacher-as-researcher" these days—too packaged. People buy back into the very system that shuts them down. That immediately eliminates the critical perspectives that we're working on, I'm afraid. But I'm still convinced that if enough people do this, we could get to a point of seeing at least a bigger clearing for us.

We liked Beth's image of a "bigger clearing." It connected us to Greene's (1986b) plea for the creation of "spaces where dialogue can take place and freedom can appear." It also reminded us of Huebner's (1987) urging us to "work intentionally at the social fabric that surrounds those of us who are called to be teachers." And the image also extended Kevin's wish to see "further and bigger."

Our discussions surrounding Katherine's dilemma with her student teachers encouraged her to explore issues of control and prescription within her work at the reading clinic, her work with her first-graders, and her relationships with her colleagues. She began to weave connections and analyses among these situations and the "social fabric" that bound them all.

The second dilemma that Katherine presented helped us all to "work intentionally." She initially spoke, in our October 4, 1987, meeting, about how our focus upon ourselves as "knowers" was helping her with her frustrations in her teaching context:

> This group breaks down the isolation for me. I feel as though I am now part of a bigger picture. This gives me a chance to talk and to think. I feel so much more confident as a teacher, as I realize that a lot of my frustration isn't all my fault. I share more readily, and I'm not so resistant to others' ideas. I was always very quiet but now I feel more comfortable with myself, more confident. What this group has done for me is help me to know that I do have something to say, that questions are something to say. So, I'm more willing to share, more outgoing, more willing to say what I think even though everyone may not agree. I feel like this group is a bridge, letting me go back and forth from myself and this group to my larger worlds and then back again.

Katherine then talked about her problems with a new first-grade teacher who kept asking her how to do everything. The new teacher was concerned that, because she had years of work experience other than teaching behind her, she would be expected to be a "perfect" teacher immediately. Katherine connected this to her experiences with the reading student teachers who had wanted absolute answers, as well as with her own feelings about having to be a "perfect" teacher. She noted her own handling of this dilemma that she saw as representative of some of the oppressive expectations as well as overt conditions with which we were struggling:

> When this teacher asks me, "what do I do?" I say, "well, this is how I do it. I don't know if this would work for you and your students." I'm practically begging her to do it her own way. Finally, last Friday, we stayed after school

to work on our new reading program which we all find frustrating. It's the usual problem with basal readers. I said that I really didn't know what I was going to do with it, and this seemed to allow her to speak up, to offer her own ideas. We worked together for an hour and a half to figure out how we could work together to make this work for us. It was good.

I realized, from our work here, and now especially from the carton episode, that as much as I have felt inadequate, and as much as I thought I was encouraging her to do it her own way, I still might have been contributing to her feelings of inadequacy by playing the "expert" teacher with years of experience. I could have been oppressive to her, just as I have been oppressed by others telling me the "right" way to do things.

We spent some time in this session talking again of Freire's warning about "malefic generosity." We had become acutely aware of how any of our behaviors as teachers, as educators who are expected to have the answers, could so easily lapse into subtle versions of this tendency to help others in ways that would merely encourage them to become more like ourselves. We also discussed the ways in which we, at the same time, had internalized the expectations of those above us in the hierarchy and thus had often conformed to reified conceptions of "good teaching" that were based on systems of "expert" observation, evaluation, and research of our activities.

As Katherine noted, particularly for elementary teachers, the majority of whom are women, these expectations are difficult for teachers to challenge because of the marginalization of their voices within the hierarchy of most school organizations. The danger as Katherine described it was that women teachers often asserted their voices and expertise in an authoritative way, over the only other people with whom they had daily contact and some control—their students and novice teachers.

Katherine's concerns were beginning to reflect her increasing awareness of the complex dynamics that resulted from the historical residues of the patriarchal nature of school organizations and the disenfranchisement of teachers through the "feminization of teaching."[1] Her remarks especially alluded to the concepts of "burnout" and "deadwood" that Freedman, Jackson, and Boles (1982) found as most often used to describe women elementary school teachers' sense of frustration and anger with their jobs. Their two-year study pointed to these concepts as easy scapegoating approaches that blamed the individual teacher for her feelings of frustration and failure. Their work, as well as the work of many others in education, points to the necessary examinations, not of individual teachers' inadequacies, but rather of the contradictory demands made upon teachers by the very structures of the schools and societies within which they teach.

At the same time, by providing the space for Katherine to struggle with the details of her daily teaching life that were leading to her sense of frustration and bewilderment, our collaborative group anchored such examinations and prevented them from becoming abstract and distanced from her everyday experience. By focusing upon and revealing the details, difficulties, and contradictions of our lives as educators, we were attempting to "open up the other half of social reality which has been ignored in studies of public life" (Weiler 1988, 62).

At our December 13, 1987, meeting, Katherine shared with us her extensions of our discussions about her dilemma with the new teacher. Beth had commented on the points of dissonance that our last discussion had raised for her, and she noted that these points of dissonance might in fact be what kept our group going, in the sense of our wanting to know and caring about one another's battles with these recurring stings. She was anxious to hear what Katherine was now thinking about her situation with this new teacher, and she also was beginning to compare some of her own feelings as district evaluator to those of the new teacher. As Beth noted, "I just can't wait to get here to be able to talk about all these points that keep emerging." She then commented:

> I've noticed that when I sit down to write in my journal, I'm usually frustrated. I mean, it feels like I need the dissonance to initiate the reflection.

Katherine responded:

> You all know that I don't write much, or at least not like the rest of you do in this group. But, finally, a few weeks ago, I thought, maybe I'm going to do it. In school, I'd been closing my door while the kids were at lunch, turning off the lights, just to calm down. Or I'd go to the library and sit with my headphones on. And I thought, oh gosh, I'm shutting down again. So I thought, well, maybe if I write when I feel this way—and so I've started to write again. But what I've done is that I've asked two teachers to work with me and to keep a journal. I asked two teachers who I know are feeling similar pulls, uneasiness with what's going on in school. And I've asked them to just

write down how they feel, or incidents that they want to think about having to do with school or teaching.

Given Katherine's uneasiness with journal writing throughout our endeavors, we knew that this was a major step for her, and we shared our excitement and interest with whoops and claps.

She continued:

I know. I'm excited and I can't quite believe that I'm doing this. We are writing on our own time, but in the mornings, they now are coming into my room and we talk. Sometimes it's not deep talk, but other times, we talk about our writing.

Katherine went on to describe the ways in which each of them wrote of frustrations, especially with the rigid administrator who they all felt contributed to their sense of powerlessness in the school. Katherine described how she even began to research "theories of frustration," as she called them, in order to have a conceptual framework within which to view her responses to the situation. She said that what she found within her own journal writing was her ability to make sense of her state of mind, her feelings. Her "research" allowed her to focus on her points of dissonance within her school; then, as she worked with the two teachers, she was able to look beyond the boundaries of her own stance to see the ways in which others were experiencing similar or different responses.

Katherine also discussed, in this meeting, that she now had begun to see the journal writing as a form of research. She had viewed our meetings and discussions as such for quite a while, but, until her work with the two teachers in her school, she had not been able to experience the writing as a possible form of research too. As she had noted earlier, "it's very hard to not always think of research as someone else's work that you look up in books." Here, she admitted that the hardest part of considering her own writing as a possible component of a research process had been in feeling that what she had to say could be of any possible consequence. Katherine had not wanted to speak in "someone else's voice" and now, as she said, "I'm finally able to speak with my own."

Katherine than elaborated on her understandings thus far, in her collaborative work with the two teachers, of some of the layers of assumptions that she had built up for herself as teacher:

118

One of the teachers wrote in the same kind of feeling framework that I did. The other one described more external events that were going on in the school. I thought that each would approach the writing like I did. And then I saw that it was wrong of me to try to fit her into my preestablished framework. I could only see this as I looked back over the writing that we did and thought about our discussions. But what really connected for me in my writing was my frustration with the teacher who kept asking me what to do.

I had found out that the principal had encouraged her to come in and watch me teach. He finally told me about this, saying that she was having a difficult time fostering independence in the kids. She was mothering them too much, he said. He said that I mothered but did not smother. What I finally realized was maybe, as much as I worried lately about imposing on her, that I was letting her do this to me, do the same thing that she let her students do to her. I thought that I was encouraging her to figure her own way, but maybe by offering my way, I was still leading her too much, still unconsciously encouraging her to do it my way. This really gets all combined and sticky, doesn't it?

We agreed that this was not an either-or proposition. As Kevin noted, "I guess you could be imposing your own notions without realizing it and, at the same time, be allowing her to impose her stuff on you!"

Katherine continued:

And so, I finally said to her the other day, when she asked me about a new student she had just received into her class, "What would *you* do?" And she rattled off all sorts of good ideas, and I said, "That sounds fine to me." And that was it. There it was. I let her answer her own question, let her listen to her own voice.

And it was all this stuff that we have been doing together that finally allowed me to see what I was doing, to see that I was replicating the same controls that had been put on me. I realized too that part of me was reacting to my own situation when I first started to teach first-graders and I was given the curriculum. It has taken me a long time to realize how angry I was about the given-ness of it all. And so I wanted this woman to see how much better she could do if she could know her own strengths. And yet I wasn't really helping her find her own, I was telling her mine.

Marjorie responded immediately to this:

This actually was the same thing as the carton for me. It reminds me of when I was watching the other state mentor give a problem-solving workshop. The teachers left feeling worse than when they came in because they felt inadequate. It was as though the workshop confirmed their own powerlessness because the answers were in the box, according to the "expert's" stance.

Katherine:

It never would have occurred to me without our research that maybe the principal was trying to "deskill" this teacher, even though he talked about her observing me as a way to make her better. But that really put me into the "expert" stance and I look at how long it's taken me to realize the dangers in that, for her and for me. And besides, it was still his assessment, as principal, that she was deficient. Maybe she never would have felt that so strongly, had he not devalued her "mothering" approach.

Kevin:

This is so tricky. How do you not fall into these situations? Because that's how so many programs for teacher development or effectiveness are set up now. The whole idea of "mentor teacher" for example. Or how the teachers in the elementary school always look to me for answers because I am the "expert school psychologist." And what I've been realizing for a while too is that response is also connected to the fact that I'm a man. Wonder if they'd ask me as much if I were a woman psychologist?

Cheryl:

All of this is so connected, and filled with danger. If we just accept the organization as it is, then we're accepting all kings of inequitable situations and even repeating them with our students. And yet, I still feel a pull between having a model as a building image and having a model of teaching, or whatever, as a prescription, a demand, an expectation. What do we do when we are being evaluated on that prescribed model?

Beth had been listening quietly to this extended discussion; she finally broke her silence, and in so doing, pointed to the contradictions that still existed between our explorations and the structures that continued to bind our vision and our actions. Even after we had spent so much time in identifying and grappling with our various points of dissonance, Beth's interruption of our discussion pointed to the stasis that she was feeling with our work:

I'm still having such a difficult time in my new job as district evaluator, having a hard time zeroing in on evaluating programs and the people in them whom I've worked with as a teacher for almost twenty years. I wish I had someone nearby to stand by me and show me how to do it, like the apprentices that Schön describes in *The Reflective Practitioner*. I can't find it in a book or a person, and so I feel absolutely lost. I can't find anywhere to go. You're the only people I can say this to without being judged incompetent. And so, Katherine, I feel like I am just like this woman who kept coming to you. What I feel is just what I think this woman is coming to you for.

Marjorie responded:

You're looking for a carton?

Beth:

Yes! And I realize all that we're saying about emancipatory aspects of ourselves as teachers-researchers, and yet in this new situation, I want a carton! I had a model of "teacher." I took a model (not sure which label to put on it in today's jargon), but I had a model and took those qualities or characteristics and let myself come out. I haven't been able to find a model yet for this job. I can't find anything to grab onto.

Beth than compared her feelings to those of the student and in-service teachers with whom Katherine and Marjorie had been working. As we discussed these situations in which people felt that they needed models or guides or right answers with which to frame their work, we also acknowledged that we all had felt the same needs as we began new positions. We talked of Schön's (1983) point that novices do not have the experience to even allow them to reflect-in-action in an immediate and fluid manner; thus, the notion of an apprentice being able to watch a professional think and reflect-in-action was a crucial experience that we all felt was lacking in teachers' preparation. None of us had experienced student teaching in these ways, because, as Cheryl said, "There was no need to reflect. It was all laid out for you!"

A crucial point emerged for us all as we listened to Beth's feelings of uneasiness and frustration with her perceived need for a "carton." We understood that those feelings emerged from a complex intersection of externally constructed as well as internally imposed expectations. Cheryl noted:

Actually, I think it's O.K. that we all use models or guides or whatever as we begin to learn a new job, especially such a complex process as teaching. I guess the tension comes in when you are never given a chance to really think about that model or to change parts of it, once you get started and can see where it might not work. And also, there are tensions if someone tells you that this is the model to use. Choice is a big part of this, yes?

Marjorie responded:

I even think that what you choose to do to deal with your frustrations is part of what we are about here. Beth, you could have chosen just to follow what the person before you did. At least that would have been some model for you to follow, since you are feeling so lost right now. But you didn't choose to do that. You at least knew that wasn't how you wanted to do this job. Instead, you have brought your frustrations to us—not that you expect us to know the answers. [Laughter, as Beth says, as an aside, "Well, I was sort of hoping. . . ."] But at least you know that you have a space where you can begin to look at all the reasons for your feelings. That's some form of emancipation, even in a tiny form, don't you think?

Beth answered:

I guess, in some ways, that I get so hung up on trying to do our stuff in my world that I forget to look at the ways in which we really are a model for what I'm looking for. I say that I don't know what to do, but if I just give myself the time and space, either in my journal or here, I can see that I do know what to do. I'm just still having trouble holding on to this when I leave here. I can remember Kevin saying the same thing a long time ago, when we began. I just feel so pressed when I get into my job every morning and I'm just sure that my supervisor has one vision of how I should do this job. And I still want his approval, even as I know, I truly know, that I see this job differently from how he sees it. Katherine, it's the same feelings that you've been dealing with in your situation, yes?

Cheryl commented:

I think that what our group has given me are the tools, so to speak, to go back to my work with the LD kids and to look at what I'm doing with them. And I'm only trying to share the tools with the teachers whom I'm working with now in my research, to see if we can become more aware of our reactions to our kids, to give them more time and opportunity to think and respond. So, our processes are a form of tools, they're not answers for everyone. But if you have the right tools for the job, as my father always says to me, it sure makes the task easier.

Katherine then responded:

Yes, we do have similar feelings and difficulties, I think. But, Cheryl, you just said it. The image of tools is good, especially in the contexts that we have to try all this. They'll love the image, even though the ones who see their jobs as being in charge might not understand how we're talking about it! With the idea of our processes as tools, it no longer matters that I did it right.

I have been frustrated because, for so many years, I just took my actions from a book or from what someone else told me I should be doing. But when we kept going as a group, and when I started to write with the two teachers, and when I could ask the new teacher, "What do you think?", I finally could see that the point is not *how* you go about it, about understanding things in deeper ways, but *if* you go about it!

Beth thought for a while, and then asked:

So you're saying that you've seen some ways of working with people, sharing some of your concerns and frustrations and looking at those closely, that you might not have seen before? You've saying that I'll probably be able to see some ways too? [Laughter, as Beth looked at us with raised eyebrows.] You think that this is really our research? [We nodded, laughing some more, and yet gently supporting Beth as she continued her role as insistent questioner.] And so you're saying that you wouldn't have done any of this if this group hadn't been?

Katherine:

Absolutely not! I couldn't even have considered any of these things. I'd still be sitting in the dark with my headphones on!

Beth, who until this point in our collaborations, might have described herself as more vocal, more prone to asking questions than anyone else in our group, responded most directly to Katherine's emerging questions and her sense of urgency about the very asking of those questions that now infused our meetings. A subtle change in the tone as well as direction of our discussions resulted from this shift in Katherine's accelerated participation in our dialogue, and in Beth's willingness to listen to Katherine's grapplings with her particular frustrations and questions as possible illumination of her own.

In a sense, our meetings enlarged to include Katherine's verbalization of her perspectives on issues to which she had previously listened and responded in quiet and often private ways. The boundaries of our collaboration were expanding and shifting to accomodate voices and questions and perspectives that were just emerging. In the connections that Beth especially was making with Katherine's approaches to her situation's complexities, we all were made aware of the ways in which we could encourage and enable one another in our attempts to avoid the exclusions and spots of blindness that particularized outlooks within our "safe place" might harbor.

Beth struggled with the points of dissonance that had emerged as she confronted the contradictions within the "carton of knowledge" of her evaluator position. She was "not prepared," as she said, for these stings that had penetrated so swiftly and so deeply as she attempted to integrate herself into her role as evaluator. She wrote voluminous journal entries during this time, continuing to use her journal to confront, to ponder, even to scream on occasion.

Even before that December meeting, Beth had become aware of her stings of dissonance. Her December 1, 1987, journal pointed to the pain that she already was acknowledging:

I've been thinking about what happens in the classroom for me, and I suspect for many, many others. The environment I set up [in earlier teaching] was one that allowed me to be myself, allowed me to be heard. I know I allowed others to be heard and perhaps that's the bigger picture. But I can see I no longer have that type of environment and it is difficult for me. I don't think it is the need to go back and be a teacher again but to find a space that allows me to be me, to feel that what I have to say is important. The only place there is for me where I can be me to the greatest degree is our teacher-researcher group. I wonder if in administration that environment is dropped because of self-interests taking a priority, because of the fear of being shown as an incompetent, because of a false self built upon successfully landing a job? I do not own this job yet and cannot "see" what that could mean. The struggle is either with me always having to ask, or with the subtle controls emanating from those who are my superiors. I just have to keep looking at all this.

Beth's journal entry of January 11, 1988, reflected her changes in perspective and interaction within our group as well as her continuing struggle to illuminate the sources and intersections of her externally and internally constructed expectations:

The biggest change for myself that I have felt in a long time came from our last research meetings where Katherine went on about her project with the two teachers and her situation with the new teacher in school. Here I was looking for dependency but wanting independence inside. Her scenarios helped me to see this in myself, and I know that it's a constant battle. Her actions have helped me to stand taller and to not fear it all so much.

I wrote back to Beth in a dialogue journal entry of January 29, 1988:

I can see how you are struggling with all aspects of this job right now. The job itself seems to bring lots of issues to the surface for you. And I know that you fight that shutting down and shutting out that the pressures sometimes force you to do. You talk about trying to resist the compartmentalized, sequential, logical aspects of your job as the only ways to do it, and yet, sometimes, maybe your shutting down is an intuitive way of protecting your sanity, of knowing where you have to stop pushing, for the moment, anyway! You keep trying to pose evaluation to your supervisors as more than packaged, measured, and timed versions of knowledge. You *are* making the connections between your own points of dissonance and the ways in which you want to do this job rather than *have* to do this job, don't you think?

At our meeting of January 31, 1988, in response to our writings and to the discussions from the previous meetings, Beth told Katherine of the impact that her emerging voice had upon Beth's understanding of her own struggles with issues of authority and compliance:

Your question to that teacher, "What would *you* do?," has changed my life in some ways, I think. All I could think about was how much I was like that woman, in wanting the model to follow for my job, and in wanting approval that I was doing it "right." I know that I have been talking about the "right answer" issue for a while, but that situation really made me step back and look at myself in ways that you were seeing that woman. You saw her as dependent and unsure, and yet you also were able to see how much of her was in you, yes? That you were able to do that, finally, to see all those things in that one situation, and to act in a way that let her hear herself and you hear yourself has really had an impact on me.

Katherine responded immediately to Beth's outpouring:

Yes, *please* remember that I think I reacted to her as dependent, as annoying me on some level, because she reminded me so much of myself when I was starting as a teacher, and even years into my teaching. It's only since I've begun to have a sense of my own ability to know what to do in the classroom that I've known how much better I've been as a teacher. And now, when I had to face up to these issues, mostly because of what we have been doing here and because I couldn't deny them anymore, I knew that I couldn't stay in the dark anymore. I knew that if I did, I'd shut down completely. And so, even though I've always been so quiet, I know that I do have something to say, and so I'm becoming vocal!

We laughed, not because we doubted Katherine's enlarged "voice" but because she, in her quiet and gentle way, was speaking with a forcefulness and vigor that was new and contagious.

Beth then shared her latest discrepancy, which had emerged from her reflection upon the similarities between Katherine's new teacher and herself:

Now the thing that scares me is, if I want to be independent, stand on my own two feet and not depend on anyone else's approval for my work, for my life, then does my need for this group, or for some form of connection or collaboration destroy my independence? At the same time, too, I don't want to build a fence around my job so that the only way I can collaborate is away from it, outside it, in our group, for example, where there are no political or emotional complications as a result of my being the evaluator.

I responded:

Beth, this sounds a lot like me as I fought with the carton of knowledge and my expectations for "sameness" and "unity." It really doesn't have to mean that you will lose your sense of self here any more than it means that you have to lose it in your job. It's not an either–or proposition, I don't think. I think that I'm finally seeing ways in which this is truly a wavelike process, undulating in and out of the various contexts of our lives.

And Kevin interrupted, also challenging in ways that, as he admitted, he would not have in earlier aspects of our collaboration:

Beth, I think that you are starting to feel more who you are now, and more confident of yourself. It sounds like, before we really got into this, that maybe you never did want to explore what collaboration might mean. Remember when you withdrew from us, a little bit in your head, at least, as you told us? Maybe you were still just looking then for someone to tell you what to do, and you weren't finding that here. And now, what you're seeing is that you don't need that. You just need the place and the support where you can feel that, and see what you saw in Katherine's encounter with the new teacher. Or be able to hear that Katherine's principal can no longer tell her that she's a good girl! She doesn't need that anymore. There were no answers

126

there, just examples. But you could draw from that to look at your own situations.

So our collaboration isn't making us the same, just as Janet pointed out. That's a real strength in all this. We're just aware of so much more, but it doesn't even have to be the same stuff, for each of us, that we're aware of!

Marjorie joined in:

I'm finally beginning to believe that you begin to know you're a person with possibilities of acting in charge of your own life when you don't need approval from everyone! Or if you can see ways in which to act around the stuff that's holding you down. Not that we don't want to be acknowledged as persons, but that we don't depend on their approval, or permission, in order to act, or to know.

When I went to Albany a few weeks ago for another mentor meeting, I realized that I no longer felt hurt that no one seemed interested in my dissertation. I had felt hurt last summer, as I was finishing. They knew then, at that meeting, that I had done case studies of three teachers who had participated in the syllabus workshops and who were attempting to implement the syllabus requirements in their classrooms. I had so much that I wanted to share about my research, about my concerns with the varying ways in which these teachers had interpreted the state's conception and design of problem-solving, and about my own questioning now of only one way to "get it." I really felt that they should want to know about my research, that I had drawn implications that pointed to the difficulties and contradictions in implementing this new syllabus.

This time, I sat in the meeting and realized that, although no one asked about my dissertation, I knew that I had some important things to say, as a result of my research and our work here. And so, this was the first time that I spoke up at one of these large mentor meetings. I just didn't care anymore if they thought I was good, or not. I just knew that, finally, I had something to say!

I responded:

I think the differences that I might finally be seeing have to do with exploring too the differences between "authoritative discourse"—how we *should* speak or act or think, based upon someone else's constructions of knowing and doing, and my own sense of authority—that I do have a perspective and my connections to the world are the points from which I *can* speak. The trick is always to be open in that perspective, to see that there might be yet other ways of seeing or talking too, and yet to see the differences between authoritarian and authority. And to know that it's really easy to slide back into the "carton." It's really difficult not to slide back, and I'm still struggling with it, but I think it's the difference between speaking *with* authority, hearing and knowing your own voice, rather than *from* a position of authority that is not necessarily your own voice.

Beth had listened quietly to all of our points. She then said, with a little smile, "I guess that I need to get vocal too!"

The journal, both monologue and dialogue, continued to serve as Beth's sounding board in her attempts to become vocal. She wrestled with her questions, which she had shared with us from the beginning, but which she now also viewed in light of the questions and dialogue and situations of our group members. She noted this change in her perspective by remembering her initial insistence on transferring our collaborative processes to her work situations, both in the classroom and then in her administrative role. She no longer was as insistent upon this immediate transference, instead preferring to acknowledge that, as she noted in a February 22, 1988, journal entry:

> these things take time. I can't rush it or expect others to want to do what I want to do. I'd package them, and yet that's what I've been most afraid of, and what I'm struggling the most against in my job!

Beth also began to address directly the sources for her need for approval and her tendencies to deny her own wants in deference to others' needs and demands. In her journal, she began to note the situations in her work relationships with her supervisor and with the teachers, who now viewed her in a different light, that especially highlighted these points of dissonance. Throughout the late winter and early spring months of our second year together, Beth kept returning to the beginnings of her job as evaluator to see ways in which she had formed relationships that ensured her silence. As she contrasted these origins with her present interests in becoming vocal, Beth also provided us with examples that, like the "carton of knowledge" itself, illuminated the depth of our various layers of assumptions, and the difficulties that we all encountered, as Beth noted, "when we try to climb out of that damn carton!"

She wrote extensively about one particular situation that "jumped out at her," in retrospect. From Beth's March 16, 1988, journal entry:

> Last fall, I was given the job to "do an evaluation on final exams." The statement was obviously too broad, but being unaware of what it would entail, I said, "fine." I could only envision a box with every teacher's final

exam filed away. By November, I was realizing that this was a huge undertaking, and that the questions themselves had changed, both from my immediate supervisor and from myself as I tried to do all this work surrounding the evaluation. His question had changed to, "Let's look at final exam results compared to final grades. Determine if there is any validity or reliability with these exams." Two mammoth tasks, and I was starting to wonder why he wanted this all done. Was this something to "get" teachers with?

Beth agonized in her journal about the ways in which this evaluation project highlighted a number of her developing concerns: these concerns centered on the nature and form of her work, on the distortions and short-cuts that often were created by the multiple interests of various individuals who had a stake in this particular study, and on her relative feelings of inadequacy and fear as she attempted to juggle these competing and contradictory forces.

Beth's writing and discussion focused more and more on her feelings of being judged in all of these situations that resulted from her position as district evaluator. She had brought these issues to our March 13, 1988, meeting, and Kevin responded:

You know, even though it took me a while to adjust to being in both the high school and the elementary school, I realize that the more buildings I'm working in, the freer my role. If I were in only one role, in one school, I would probably have to struggle more with fitting in, like you all are, while, at the same time, trying to examine all the impositions that we have been looking at. I can see why you all are feeling the "cartons" maybe more than I am. I have so many bosses that I really don't have one. And I like that, I realize how much I want that independence! And I think that I can move more freely, and that, because I'm a man, as we have really been discussing lately, I have more expected autonomy than many of my female colleagues, especially in the elementary school. And especially in contrast to you, Beth, who have so many immediate constraints on whom you answer to.

Beth replied:

Yeah, what I've really been looking at lately is my definition of "boss." I realize that, for years, my definition has been "the one who tells me I'm worthy!" It's like I've had to be told this, it hasn't been from within. And now that I'm realizing this, I not only want to become "more vocal," I want to start screaming! And yet I don't want to blame anyone either. I just want to start doing it all differently.

Marjorie responded to Beth's obvious pain:

> You know, part of our whole work together, I guess, is to give us a place to even see reasons for wanting to see and act differently. It really has put us smack in the center of our stuff.

Beth talked about the importance, for her, of not feeling alone with her points of dissonance, and of the importance of the group as the fulcrum upon which she could build her connections among the issues that emerged, in theme and variation again, throughout her personal and professional life. She responded to Marjorie's comment:

> I guess that's what you mean by us being smack in the center. I can see now how much I was looking "out there" for the connections of this to my daily life. It's probably why I was so intent on creating committees and groups who would immediately do what we do. But now I see that my work first has to be where I am, where I find my own places to make my connections and feel my dissonance. Oh, how I'm knowing the dissonance now! [Once again, we laughed, all appreciating the emotions that Beth summarized so well for us.] I guess I'm in the center of trying to figure out how I can just do my job with integrity, and with a voice, finally, huh?

Extended Spaces and Voices

As much as I had spoken, even at the beginning of our collaboration, about the shifts in our perceptions of teaching and research that our attempts might necessitate, I do not think that any of us had any idea of the impending force of those shifts upon our daily work as educators. As Beth and Katherine both exclaimed, the impact and power of their individual stories upon one another's attempts to "climb out of the carton" were unexpected, painful, and yet vital examples of the interactive and reciprocal nature of our collaboration. Our varying yet equally strong reactions to Marjorie's "carton of knowledge" had precipitated further investigation into sources and manifestations of dissonance for each of us. So too had our telling of our battles to extend our voices affected our understandings of the effects of placing ourselves at the center of our collaborative research efforts.

Kevin noted that what our centering efforts did, more than anything else, was to allow him to see what he had originally hoped for, back in our formative meetings—"to see further and bigger." He elaborated on this thought in our March 13, 1988, meeting:

I can see how much our work makes us take an abstract notion like "empowerment" and look at what it means for us in what we do every day and what it might mean for the kids and teachers we work with, too. And in thinking about all of us and our different ways in which we try to make sense, like Katherine and Beth wanting to become "more vocal," I think about all of our connections now when I go to work every day. And I begin to see how some of my own reactions are the same as yours, even though I might never have thought about them that way before.

For example, I'm just really realizing how important my moving around from building to building is in terms of not getting caught up in the hierarchical stuff and power pulls that I can see happen for us all. I'm beginning to understand why I especially felt so "pulled apart" in the elementary school. I just don't want to have to be put either into the position of "expert" or of subservient and compliant worker. And those were the only two ways I was seeing there, I think.

I can now hear some of the things that get said to me in a different way, based on our discussions and work. Now when I hear someone say, "Oh, Kevin, you do such a good job," I sometimes wonder if they're really saying, "Oh, Kevin, you're such a good boy." Not that I have to deal with that to the extent that women do in terms of being "good girls" in the system, but I can see ways now that, when someone would say that, I would think, "Oh, I better keep doing the same thing. They like it." I wouldn't look beyond a comment like that like I would now.

Not looking beyond that could be really destructive. Because, in a way then, you are giving someone else the power over you without even questioning. It's easy to say this, though, but really hard for me to do, just like it's really hard for all of us.

Cheryl responded to Kevin's examples:

I really think that this whole experience now acts like a trigger for me, it triggers thoughts or connections for me when I'm caught up in my daily work. And I know that I wouldn't be doing now what I'm doing with my LD kids and with the teachers if we hadn't moved so far with this. I'm having the students do daily journals!

They can't really write much, according to most people, but they do one or two sentences for me at first. Now I can see them beginning to have a bit more confidence and certainly more interest. I keep encouraging them to write about things they know or about questions that they might have. And now that I'm interviewing and doing dialogue journal writing with three other LD teachers for my research focus, I can see how the kids' sense of confidence is tied up in having a chance to talk and write about themselves, just like the teachers! And I do think that the teachers are becoming more aware of what I call "response allowance," whether in talking or writing, and they are seeing that as important for the students and themselves.

You know, one of the teachers I'm working with in my research asked me why I keep coming to our meetings, especially now that I have these other teachers to work with. And I said, "I can't ever forget all the examples and sharing from our group that have helped me to see things in different ways." I go, I told her, because my whole self, not just my teaching, keeps changing.

Both Kevin and Cheryl, especially, had attempted to use some of the "tools," as Cheryl called them, of our collaborative efforts in their researching and teaching. Both continued to use journal writing as a way in which to interact and research with students and teachers in their respective contexts.

Cheryl wrote in a journal entry of February 10, 1988:

As I work with the LD teachers in our interactive discussions and in our dialogue journals, I realize that our group hasn't just been talking about ourselves, but has been always looking at ourselves as teachers or counselors or evaluators in relations with others. We're dealing with ourselves in the bigger picture, and yet this is very personal because, in the very nature of our work, we relate to other people, and we want to relate as humans, not as robots who can only "spit back."

I know that I keep coming back to that term, "spit back," but it just captures so much of what my own education was about and also so much of what I see special educators, especially, thinking that their work with kids has to be. I still see the "flat" answers that teachers expect from their students as a major area that those of us in special education could work on to expand our own visions of what's possible for us and for these students.

As Cheryl continued to extend the focus of her original ideas for research within our collaborative exchanges, she found herself, like all of us at this point, unable to look at her own particular situation without also thinking of the stories that we all had told. She began to call this "the personalization of curricula," as she explored the connections between the private and public worlds that our work had begun to make explicit. Cheryl knew that she now was looking and looking again at the foundations of her field which embodied the perspectives of positivist and behaviorally oriented researchers and the practices of teachers who saw themselves as implementors of these approaches within the classroom. She also knew that she was taking a minority stance within her field, and yet she proclaimed her determination, at our meeting in March 1988, not to perpetuate the "spit back" mentality that she saw permeating so much of special educators' philosophical and pedagogical approaches.

Cheryl wrote, in an April 4, 1988, entry:

> By discussing issues and problems in the field and in daily teaching practice, teachers *can* become aware of what they are doing, of how well that interfaces with their philosophy, and of how they can solve their own problems and improve their services to LD youngsters. This metacognitive awareness is a first step toward determining whether our teaching *status quo* is acceptable to ourselves as teachers and to our perceptions of the role of the practitioner in the field of learning disabilities. I strongly believe that the educational community may benefit from teachers who are aware of how they personalize curricula for their students.

Cheryl was placing herself, as well as other special educators, at the center of research and teaching practices by pointing to our interactive and reciprocal relationships as a way by which teachers themselves, in relationships with their students, could determine the direction and focus of their work. She knew that this position was a difficult one to maintain, given the pressures for accountability and raised achievement scores that especially characterized her work as a special educator, and that often pushed teachers to the borders rather than to the center of these determinations.

However, in her attempts to "look differently" at her work as well as to encourage other LD teachers to engage in that viewing process, Cheryl was rejecting the notion that her work and her pedagogical approaches, imbued as they were with static conceptions of knowledge production and dissemination, were predetermined and thus impervious to teachers' changing perceptions and understandings. In a sense, Cheryl, like all of us, was searching for her own possibilities, even as she was illuminating the sources of the diminishing processes that infiltrated her work with her learning-disabled students.

Cheryl wrote of her continuing struggles to maintain her perspective in a journal entry of June 1, 1988. She wanted to see herself as centered within her teaching and researching processes even as she grappled with the day-to-day pressures of her work that impinged upon that centered position:

> I'm always having to face what I see as the lack of relevance and usefulness of standardized tests for my LD kids. After teaching for a while, and getting

disillusioned with the constant testing, I began speaking with other teachers, discussing which tests they used and how well they thought these tests accomplished their jobs, as well as how exactly they used these tests. I guess that I thought I was just not using the right ones or in the right way. Now, after our two years together, I'm thinking about them in a whole different way. There wasn't something wrong with me or the way that I was using them! And just the other day, when I was meeting with one of my research teachers, she started to show me how she now uses tests, based on our discussions of this difficult topic. She marks down where the students are when the time is up, for the state record, and then she lets them finish the test untimed to see how much they really know and can do independently. Her decisions for how much service or help they need are becoming based on what they really *can* do (untimed, as she sees it) and not on how they scored in the allotted time. Isn't this great! We really don't have to be stuck!

Kevin also had begun to speak in ways that pointed to his awareness of the centrality of his position within his work as school psychologist. Like Cheryl, he had been wrestling with the behaviorally oriented and test-based structures of traditional conceptions of his work as school psychologist. As he studied the effects of his introduction of journal writing into his counseling sessions with elementary students, Kevin, like Cheryl, was drawn especially to the possibilities that seemed inherent within these non-standard approaches to his work. These possibilities were focused not only on the processes that he was attempting to transpose from our research group into his counseling repertoire but also on his interactions among the students and the teachers with whom he was working. He had written, in a February 5, 1988, journal entry, about his increasing understandings of his position as a relational one after our sessions in which we had concentrated on the effects of "becoming vocal:"

I think that after six years, I am finally developing my own "voice" as a psychologist. I used to just play off of what others said and just restate and agree with them. But now, more and more, I still listen, but then express my true feelings and opinions. I think that I have good instincts, and I'm learning to trust them more, and to express myself more forcefully. Well, maybe not forcefully, as much as persistently!

As Kevin became more and more involved with the writing of his students in his counseling sessions, he also made concerted attempts to involve the children's classroom teachers in his new approach. He always had talked with the elementary teachers about the children whom they had referred to him, but, as he had noted earlier in our discussions, the teachers had often talked to him as the "expert" or as the one "in charge." Kevin had been expressing his developing understandings of the gender-related aspects of this pattern of interaction, especially as our group had worked through the implications of the "carton of knowledge" and of the processes of becoming vocal. In his research, he now was attempting to bring the teachers into the center of their discussions by involving the teachers in his focus on the students' writing. As they became more familiar with Kevin's approaches with the writing, which included encouraging the children to choose their own topics for writing within each counseling session, some of the teachers began to bring samples of his clients' classroom writing to Kevin for discussion.

The teacher of a fourth-grade child, whom Kevin had been seeing for problems with his negative self-image and poor adjustment from a parochial to public school setting, approached Kevin with one of the child's in-class writing assignments. Although Kevin preferred that the children's writing in class be of the same non-assignment variety as his counseling writing episodes, he was pleased with the teacher's heightened sensitivity to the emotions that were reflected in this child's piece of writing:

the skelton who fell apart

Once there was
a skelten that was very
lonely. The children were
afraid of him so he had no
friends.
He went out to find a
friend. But he never
found one. So he kept on
looking and after he started
to hate his self. So
he starterd to cry.
And one by one
his bones
started

to fall apart. But
before he noticed he was
in pieces. And if you
walk right past where
he fell apart you can
still here him crying.

Kevin showed us this child's writing, anonymously, not only for its poignant emotions but also to discuss his evolving relationship with the child's teacher. As a result of Kevin's attempts to inform and involve the teachers in their students' writing in the counseling process, this child's teacher had developed an interest in the child's writing, from an academic as well as a reflective perspective. When she brought this story to Kevin, the teacher's comment to him was: "I've never read anything by a kid that expresses how he feels better than this."

While Kevin's research focus was more on the children's writing as a chronicle of their therapy with him, he also was aware that including their writing in his discussions and consultations with the teachers heightened their awareness and sensitivity to the children and their particular problems. As Kevin noted at our May 15, 1988, meeting:

> I knew that I wouldn't want to use the kids' writing as the main focus of my consultation with the teachers, because, although I did share emerging themes in the writing with them, I still wanted to maintain the children's options to choose their topics in our sessions. It had taken me a while to come to this issue of choice, and I didn't want the teachers to "assign" topics to them in class as a follow-up to what we did in counseling, as some of them did not agree with my point of encouraging the children to choose themselves whatever they wanted to write about. I did want to share the research of people like Graves and Calkins with them, but I knew that could not be my crusade here.
>
> I do think that the teachers started to think about this issue of choice, though, and I definitely felt that our talks changed the nature of our relationship. I no longer was the "expert." I was more like a co-investigator, because I was doing with the kids something that they did with them too—the writing. I think that my work wasn't so mysterious and distant to the teachers this way.

Kevin's research had begun in our collaborative efforts, but now extended not only into his counseling with the children but also into his daily interactions with the teachers, the parents, and the administrators in his schools. He was beginning to know that, like Katherine, he did have something to say, based on research that he had initiated and implemented as school psychologist. Although Kevin, like all of us at the beginnings of our pursuits, had had difficulty in imaging that his research could "count," he now spoke with a voice centered in his own researching experiences, rather than from the research of others, from the distanced and second-hand voices of those whose research findings he then was to implement. Kevin now spoke in his own voice about the possibilities of writing as a counseling tool that elementary school psychologists should consider.

Like each of us, Kevin through his researching efforts had tried to place himself, his students, and the teachers of those students at the center of these processes. He, like Cheryl, was working to nudge from the center of his work the standardized and test-oriented procedures that constantly threatened to muffle the voices of his students, the teachers, himself. As Kevin remarked during our May 1988 meeting:

> I could really see the differences in the kids' writing when I encouraged them to choose what they wanted to write about. I guess I've given myself a few choices now too. I feel like I'm more connected to the students and the teachers too.

Two Steps Forward, One Step Back

As our collaborative group moved into our third year of meetings and discussions, we all could say, as Kevin had, that we felt more connected, both to one another and to the issues that intertwined our collaborative and individual lives as educators. However, we still could not say that we had resolved our points of dissonance or that we had come to painless closure against any of the stings that had erupted throughout our interactions. Being more connected also meant that we were more aware, more conscious, not only of our own discrepancies but also of the stings that signaled dissonance in our points of intersections among the individuals and institutions that formed our educators' lives.

The repetitious themes of time, of uncertainties, of multiple layers, including contradictory demands in our daily lives, still competed for our attention and our loyalties. We persevered in juggling our schedules so that we might meet again and again, to explore and confront these complexities. We all stumbled upon more layers of assumptions, even as we were scrambling for vantage points from which to gain perspective on the layers that we just had excavated. The movements of our individual and collective investigations could be described, at best, as recurring. For every two steps forward, as Marjorie said, we seemed to go back at least one. She wrote of the sinuous nature of her own explorations in a journal entry of March 12, 1988:

> Now I'm involved in teaching a science methods course for undergraduates. It's different from the workshops because the students do assignments and will receive a grade for whatever/however I hold them accountable. At first, assignments seemed unnecessary—the students seemed fascinated with this new approach of problem-solving and agreed that it made sense. They loved the activities. It was only when they tried to write their first lesson plans that some of them began to grapple with their own preunderstandings about what it means to teach science. Yes, content, facts, that's really what counts, they told me. It's fine to do some hands-on to motivate the kids as long as you precede and follow it up with the "right" explanation, the facts! Oh no, here was all of my old stuff, and I still felt on shaky ground with the new perspectives that I had been developing, as a result of my research with the three teachers and with our collaborative group!

Marjorie told us of the two students who came to her after class and who were really trying to fit the problem-solving approaches into the structures of the traditional lesson plan. She and the students "thought out loud," as she put it, about the contradictions embedded in the two approaches, and tried to figure out ways of still doing the problem-solving with students without contorting its processes into behavioral objectives that called for a predetermined outcome. Marjorie continued her reflections about this episode in her journal:

> I think that I made a breakthrough in my own thinking here too. I realized that, finally, I didn't really care about the end product—the lesson plans—with the students. It was the process, the struggling with the mess, the naming of the discrepancies that I really wanted. Because of my conversations with the students, I decided not to grade the lesson plans. This is such a feeling of freedom for me that's finally happening. I knew that I couldn't give them a model lesson plan when they requested one, because, just like them, I didn't have one, I couldn't contort the process to conform to the end-product mentality. In some sense, I realize that I was asking them to

grapple with stuff that I never had grappled with as a science teacher. I guess this seems like a small step, but it is such a big one for me, given my whole rootedness in prescription. Now my fears center on gaining confidence— what if I think now that this is the only "right" way and I lose the mess that I'm now able to share?

Two steps forward, one step back. We all felt the waves of uncertainty that Marjorie so vividly expressed, and yet, in her sharing of this episode, she also invited us to help illuminate the possible blinds spots that she feared might develop in her new "vision" of the processes that she was attempting to enact. This trust was not a dependency, a demand that others see it for us, but rather was an exchange among us, of questions and dialogue freely offered and freely received. Trust had grown from our willingness to bare our points of dissonance with one another and, together, to look and look again.

Beth also shared an example of the halting yet interactive nature of our explorations as well as of the constantly surfacing layers of assumptions that characterized our work. She told, in our meeting of May 15, 1988, of a recent conversation that she had held with a curriculum director in a local school district:

I was telling this person a little about our teacher/researcher group, and about how much our work had helped me to realize that school systems, in a way, are set up in ways, even physically, that prevent teachers from thinking and talking and reflecting. But I said to this curriculum director, "I wonder what would happen if teachers *were* given the space and time to think and to talk with one another?" And this person replied, "Oh, we don't want that to happen!"

I couldn't believe it—a walking example of what we have been critiquing and fearing and trying to figure out how to work around! She went on to make it very clear to me that those in charge don't want teachers to go beyond a certain point because then they can't control what goes on in the classroom.

I just couldn't get over this. I had really still been thinking about issues of "control" and "disempowerment" for teachers in the abstract. I mean, I just didn't think that there could be real people, who work in schools, who would actually take that stance. They might think it, or it might show up in the articles and critiques as part of what happens in a hierarchical system, but I was talking with this person! And I really thought that she cared and did her job well. And she probably does, within the limits of how she and others see it.

I'm still in shock. Why would anyone want to put limits on thinking? I sound so naive, after all that we have looked at and discussed. But it still hits me over the head like a ton of bricks. I sure can see how we can't expect that everyone will come running to join our explorations!

Beth not only was expressing her shock at this blatant statement of "control" that the coordinator was presenting but also was revealing her dismay that she could not "see it all," as Katherine had earlier bemoaned. Throughout our associations, I especially had spoken about the loneliness that I often felt in my work in academe, and had connected those feelings to the nature of the work that we, too, were attempting in our collaborative explorations. Here, Beth, also, was pointing to the relative isolation among our peers that some of our developing perspectives might create. As she noted, "I guess a lot of people want things to remain as they are. They don't like it when I start asking questions or posing alternatives."

Katherine, too, still felt, at times, that she was being "hit over the head," as Beth so graphically articulated it. Even as she now knew that she had reasons to become vocal and to raise questions, Katherine also struggled with the extent to which her voice was not welcomed or encouraged within the conversations of those who decided upon issues of curriculum, of tenure, of grade assignments, of evaluation. She had written, in a journal entry of March 5, 1988:

What's bothering me still is what's underneath the apparent. What's bothering me is not really the idea of no copy machine for teachers to use, or mice in the school, or the lack of supplies. I've finally realized that teaching is a political thing. Its politics remain under the table. I know that I have deliberately and consciously avoided this for many years. I can honestly say that I was aware of it but chose to remain removed, naive, and ill-informed. When I started in 1977, I told myself that I'd never be involved. So I taught each and every class with exactly what I was given, did exactly what I was told. I never questioned class size, supply procedures, curriculum requirements, or extracurricular demands. I volunteered for everything from spring concert, to participating in Gym night, to working in three schools with no time for a scheduled lunch period. But now I'm no longer willing to do all of that, or at least I now ask "Why?" I know that I'm different now than I used to be as a teacher, I know I'm thinking differently, I *know* that I'm involved, because teaching *is* involvement! I know my involvement, my becoming vocal, has been noticed. And I don't think they like it! But I can no longer be the teacher who just teaches what others have thought up and given name to. I'm naming things now. What about me as an *educator?* Can there be such a thing, can I exist?

140

The years of pain and the layers of assumptions through which Katherine, like the other members of our group, had waded in order to pose such questions surged to the forefront of our consciousness and our dialogues. We all, slowly and carefully at first, had begun to address the situations and our possible complicities within them that had denied us our voices. We had struggled together to create a space in which we could see and speak from our own particular positions in the world, and as we were able to "see further and bigger," we were becoming more vocal and raising shattering questions. We also were realizing that the positions in which we found ourselves, among the controlling and authoritative systems and structures that guided much of our lives as educators, could be

> actively utilized (rather than transcended) as a location for the construction of meaning, a place from where meaning is constructed, rather than simply the place where a meaning can be discovered, . . . a place from which values are interpreted and constructed rather than as a locus of an already determined set of values. (Alcoff 1988, 435)

And so we have begun to know, through our questions and our dialogues and our struggles with our individual points of dissonance, "agency as opposed to passivity." As Katherine put it, "I like that feeling, even though it's also incredibly painful!"

We have come to value, more than ever, our positions as educators, understanding that those very positions from which we speak can enable us to create the meanings and relationships that could validate us all, across our differences. We also now see that our knowing comes in the small spaces, in the cracks between the mandates and our chosen actions within our daily teaching and counseling and administering.

We continue to value our ever-growing capabilities to "persistently interrupt" one another, to point out overlapping issues or contradictions in our pursuits. These interruptions are one manifestation of our action to affect our lives. Although our enlarged capacities to challenge rather than only to agree with one another have developed within the boundaries of our collaborative support, those capacities have extended our ability to affect our worlds. As Katherine noted in our September 25, 1988, meeting:

I think that my question, "What can I do?" that I posed last year so much still came out of a sort of hopeless stance. I've been thinking a lot about what has happened to me over the past two years since we've been meeting. And when we started, it was more, "Who am I?" And then, last year, it was more like, "Here I am, now listen to me!" And I know that had to be part of "becoming vocal," as I called it, but I think that maybe I had to go through all that, you know, find myself, and then, feeling, "well, now I've found myself, you better find me!" [Much laughter again, as Katherine acted out her "progressions," as she called them.]

And now, I think I'm asking myself that question, "What can *I* do?" and it's more focused on my abilities and responsibilities to act. It just isn't looking at someone else and saying, "Now, here are the problems, what are you going to do about this?" And what I now think, too, is that you can't expect everyone to come along with you on this, you know what I mean? You can't expect everyone to want to take this journey, and I think that, for a while, that's what I was expecting to happen around me.

Marjorie responded:

Yes, I can see how initially you can think that they all have to come on the journey too, or you won't be able to move either, that you'll have to stay where you are, be blocked. It's really hard to see this, that we can move, go on the journey, as you say, Katherine, and that everyone else doesn't have to come along. Sure would be easier if they would!

We all found that this balancing point continued to be a difficult one to maintain. As we had felt movement and a sense of agency developing within our explorations, we had taken these expectations into our classrooms and offices. Part of our collective space had become a forum where we now shared the "persistent interruptions" not only of one another but also of our educational settings, which continued to provide enough dissonance to dispel any sense of smooth and linear movement within our work.

As Beth had noted in our May 15, 1988, meeting, however, the group had given her a space within which to stand, to view, and to speak:

I think that this is a process of constantly moving back and forth, in and out. As you always say, Janet, this really provides a dramatic juxtapositioning! [Laughter, as Beth poked fun at one of my favorite words.] So, now we see, here's the system, the organizational structure that we work in. As we come here, we can constantly pull back a bit to look at that organizational structure and to see where we can move, ask a question, make a statement.

I can see now how much of that structure I wanted to move right into this space at first, because I didn't know anything else. But now I know differently.

"But now I know differently." As we have looked back to our beginnings, we have realized that so much of our work consists of deceptively simple acts. In our very attempts to conceive of ourselves as active agents, to perceive the shifts in our perspectives that emanated from our attempts to become researching teachers, we have had to "look and look again." That process of looking has required us to extend our vision, to "look further and bigger," beyond our individual classrooms and daily routines to the broad structures of schooling and social systems that undergird our work as educators. Simultaneously, "to look and look again" also has forced us to focus our vision. We have had to peer into the file cartons and storage bins that hold the daily records and remnants of our teaching lives, and to shake loose the accumulated dust that has layered through the years of our lectures and tests and scores.

We all have experienced pain and ambivalence and frustrations even in our very looking. The discrepancies and points of dissonance that constantly emerge within our explorations serve as persistent interruptions, but, at the same time, provide the impetus for our continuing collaboration. We do look for calm spaces within the disjunctures that we continue to address. As Cheryl put it, "It would be nice to sit and rest for a while." However, we also have come to accept that, once we began this journey, "there was no turning back," as Kevin noted. And while we also accept that we will never be finished, in that packaged sense, we also continue to derive strength and support from our gathering. We know, as Katherine pointed out, that not everyone will want to join us in our explorations, nor will share our willingness to look and look again.

At our meeting of September 25, 1988, we talked about "how we have come along on this journey," as Katherine put it. I asked the group members if they could write brief reflections about this, knowing that I wanted their own words to provide some closure to this narrative that I could not, or did not want to, provide. As I said to them:

I know that I'm asking you to do the impossible. We're not done [of course, laughter at this point], and there is no closure. But maybe at least we each could provide a brief account of where we are, from our individual perspectives, at this point in time.

Kevin responded:

Yea, I think that would be a good thing to do. But remember, Janet, we're not doing this for you now!

Although I cannot recreate in words the laughter and the warmth that surrounded these exchanges, I can share the thoughts and reflections of the members of our group at this particular juncture in our continuing collaboration. These reflections all were written in early October 1988:

Beth wrote, in part:

This "journey" is like a kaleidoscope . . . you can pick it up, turn the lens, and see something different each time. Each time I pick up this "journey" I see it differently. I see it as a friend, a solution, a salvation, an energy, and sometimes, simply as a journey, a road that will take me somewhere, or better yet, help me to walk from where I am now or help me to move beyond.

The journey started with an enthusiasm that always accompanies my beginnings. I felt a little lost and was sure I was the only one who felt this way, but, "go with it," I said. I listened when Janet first described her vision and her perceptions of this research, while I tried to feel independent and to see where I fit in. You know, "I'm a graduate student, I must think for myself." Could I possible have anything to offer? Frequently, I had to remind myself, yes, stick with it . . . you only know the beginning.

"Knowing" in retrospect is a cherished handle that I continue to stretch for, a "theme" as Janet calls it. The journal writing has let me see how frequently the themes of "time" and "balancing" emerged in both my work and family responsibilities. It's also allowed me to see how much I wrestle with ever being able to be "free." The writing allowed me to have a dialogue with myself as well as with others.

I remember that, by the end of the first year together, I began to feel irritated. "O.K., so now what?" What possibly could we learn from this experience in another year? I re-committed myself, though, knowing how much had already happened. Even though it was getting more difficult to work out time, I wanted to "see." This was now research for me. The changes in the next year were more subtle. It seemed the level of our conversations went deeper; the water was colder, more refreshing and yet still turbulent. We listened more intently, we recognized that we could not be the "answer" but that we played an important part in the bigger picture, whatever that may be.

The road goes on, I know. The "journey" has become a walk down a dry, dusty, dirt road lined with a variety of green trees and small wildflowers at the edge. I know for sure that somewhere ahead there will be a picnic table on the side of the road where we will meet and laugh and talk . . . and then we'll move on.

Kevin wrote:

When I think about our collaborative work during the last two years, I become flooded with images and feelings about the changes I've gone through, my dissertation process, the support I feel from the group, and the strength I've gained in the process. I've become, along with the other group members, a creator of meaning. I take a more active role in my professional life, and probably also in my personal life because of the reflective process.

Many times during the last two years, I've felt like I was in the "mess" and not really sure of the direction, although I've never worried about that and I've been comfortable from the start with the ambiguity of it all. In the beginning, I trusted the insight of others, and later my own insight too, to keep us going.

Three different layers of change come to the surface as I write. The first is the writing itself and my discovery of the power of writing and how writing provided release and reflection. This discovery of my own writing voice led to another layer of change as I encouraged the elementary school children whom I saw in individual counseling to write. Many times, their writing, even the writing of the youngest ones, clearly reflected deep feelings and worries. The third layer of change has been the complete support and gentle challenge that characterizes our group. We've been through much obvious personal change: marriage, new houses, job changes, pregnancy, and graduations. But we've been through just as many subtle internal changes. My commitment to the process, to our collaborative work together, has continued to grow and is much stronger now than at that picnic table over two summers ago.

Cheryl wrote, in part:

Considering where and how I have traveled, since becoming a participant in our teacher-researcher group, my resource room at school comes to mind. I think of aspects of my teaching that I consider part of a process of positive and continuing struggle and growth. Having my LD students presenting and participating in their IEP (Individual Educational Plan) conferences, getting away from demanding finished products from the students and instead asking for demonstrations of understanding of material, allowing my students to do independent or cooperative work where possible—these are some of the changes that have quietly crept into my teaching. But there is a question that has been gently floating in the back of my mind for a while. How have I been able to make such substantive changes in my teaching methods and materials while developing my teaching philosophy and coming to terms with my position on educational issues? I think that part of the answer to those questions lies in the effect our research has had on my personal struggles. Our research has allowed me to realize that it is useful to struggle, that the problems and issues confronting us are worthy of our long-term and continuous thought and action. As we have been able to postpone using other people's "right" resolutions in our search, we have been our own living examples of teachers coming to terms with the tension that is part of life. The willingness to struggle, to forego closure, to be "comfortable with reasonable doubt," as Huebner said, are personal acquisitions and outgrowths of the research that we do together.

And Katherine wrote, in part:

Our work in the teacher/researcher group has given me the opportunity to step back and question my motives, philosophies, desires, and responsibilities as "teacher." It has given me the strength to ask the question "who am I?," knowing that by questioning, I was actively choosing to grow and change. As a result of my question, many "tried and true" procedures and mandated techniques for classroom teaching no longer worked for me. I could no longer follow set ways for time management in my classroom but began to allow my own ways of teaching to come through. It also was an honest realization on my part that I was not as comfortable with journal writing as most of the other members of our group. But their acceptance of my individuality allowed me to grow even stronger in my own personal acceptance of myself as teacher, researcher, and person. As I started to feel, "look who *I* am!" I wanted to share the "new me," my new confidences, my realities. I joined a Teachers' Committee and met with the principal to discuss problems faced by the faculty. These meetings turned to gripe sessions, dead ends, and *no's*. I don't blame anyone for what happened. We, the teachers, just continued to act in the expected ways, with the principal as the authority, and we didn't look to see what ways *we* could begin to act differently.

But having the group and our work together helped me to realize that "emancipation" cannot be forced on others. Forcing anything brings resentment. My confidences and experiences are not the same as my colleagues. Therefore, I cannot expect that they will want to share the journey, as our group has done, because we have different roads, different journeys. So my question now is "what can I *do*?" that is constructive and enlightening for me, but might not be for others. This is perhaps the most difficult because the action taken on my part must represent me but also allow for the differing perspectives of others. Perhaps there are two paths on my journey: the path of the individual self (me as teacher) and the path of the collective group (teachers). I have many questions about what to "do" and how to "do" it. My participation in our teacher/researcher group helped me to begin my journey. I hope that it will help me to continue.

146

And Marjorie wrote:

Although I accepted the invitation to participate in this project to explore emancipatory possibilities, I really did not expect the form it has taken. I expected a feeling of being set free and/or an inner surge of strength and confidence. Instead, I feel confused, but willing to keep searching, and absolutely convinced that the only thing that I can change (or need to worry about changing) is me. I've managed to put away others' cartons, but still I'm discouraged at times by the cartons that I create for myself. Probably the most tangible evidence of emancipation for me comes in an internalized conviction that there truly is no "right way" to do this and an acceptance of not being done. I see my job far less as goals to be achieved than as research. There are lots of obstacles to my accomplishing what I think I should be doing—both in the structures of the institution in which I work and within myself. But I now find myself thinking that my *real work* is trying to think about it all differently. The group is very important to me. Understatement! The feelings of futility that come over me at times when I look at how schools go about the task of educating children are surpassed when I reflect on what I have seen happening to people here. When Katherine talked, at our last meeting, about holding some of our future meetings in her new home, I *knew* beyond a doubt that something had happened to each of us. No one hesitated even a split second about committing to future meetings. We are, finally, a place in which to touch and know that things can be/are different.

And I wrote:

I had no idea, at that picnic, what this would become for us. I wish that I could capture the sense of movement that has grown throughout our work. I wish, most of all, that I could capture the joy that we share. We have struggled so much, each of us in different ways, but how we have laughed too! That's what I wish that we could share with others—not the same journeys, as Katherine said, but the joy.

We now understand, in ways that we had not dreamed possible at that summer picnic, that to become challengers requires the active constructions of our own worlds and our own possibilities even as we look to see and to challenge the forces and structures that prevent them. We now view our collaborative researching efforts as a point of mediation, a balancing place from which to launch our next questions, to pose our persistent interruptions, to explore new points of dissonance. We have come to realize that we, like all those who wish to become challengers, will have to learn to love the questions, . . . to realize that there can be no final agreements or answers, no final commensurability. And we have been talking about stories that open perspectives on communities grounded in trust, flowering by means of dialogue, kept alive in open spaces where freedom can find a place. (Greene 1988, 134)

EPILOGUE

"We're Not Done Yet": Problems and Possibilities in Creating Spaces and Finding Voices

That our research group continues to meet indicates the support and the challenges that we find within our collaboration. Our desire to further explore the possibilities of our collaborative teacher-researcher stances implies as well our willingness to "remain in the mess." We know that this slippery vantage point is a precarious but necessary position from which to acknowledge and confront the sources of our various stings of dissonance. However, as a result of our collaborative efforts, we have come to believe that any attempts to change school structures, or our relationships to them, that we find to be oppressive or stifling must originate in "the mess" of our daily work as educators.

Our continuation also implies the evolving nature of the very processes by which we attempt to examine and to further our explorations of the unseen forces in schools and society that affect who we are as educators, as teacher-researchers. At the same time, our collaboration signifies a form of action upon our worlds, and alludes to the possibilities of other constructions and contexts in which educators might take action to create collaboration where "dialogue can take place and freedom can appear."

Thus, as we work through our third year of discussions and research, we believe that we have been together long enough to reflect on the difficulties as well as joys of forming and maintaining a collaborative group that is committed to change and is supportive of one another through those processes. Throughout our journey, we have struggled with problems and potentials that we think are lodged within the logistics as well as within the underlying assumptions and orientations of those collaborative processes. Problems that we have identified within our collaborative attempts include the very processes and intentions of creating spaces and finding voices.

We continue to confront issues of voice, authority, and imposition within our attempts to develop interactive research perspectives in dialogue journal writing, group discussion, reflection, and collaboration; we also constantly confront those issues within the structures of our individual educational settings as we attempt to transpose our research perspectives into those settings.

We still raise questions about the possibilities of teachers becoming researchers of their own practice as well as of the institutions that frame and form that practice. We continue to explore forms of research that attempt to acknowledge the perspectives and participation of all those involved; yet we continue to be confronted by the separation of theory and practice, teaching and research, that signify the predominant end-product orientation of most of the educational settings in which we work. We wonder if the label, teacher-as-researcher, in fact contributes in subtle ways to those theoretical and practical distinctions that continue to obscure the ways in which teaching itself is a "quiet form of research" (Britton 1987). We are concerned that the application of the label *researcher* still implies the bestowing of a greater status than that of "teacher," and we worry that empowerment still is considered a reward by some, to be granted along with the rights and privileges encompassed by the title, *researcher*. While we grapple with all of these issues, we also continue to acknowledge the tensions between our desire for community and support in these explorations and the dangers of a collective unity that might veil the differences among us.

At this point, we do know that there is no one right way to enact these processes of creating spaces and finding voices, as our collaboration vividly exemplifies, and as Beth can now attest so well. Thus, we also want to present our work as one of a growing number of examples of educators who intuitively feel the importance of becoming challengers, who see few spaces in which dialogue and freedom might appear, and yet who daily forge those spaces and connections in the openings afforded during lunch duty, during faculty meetings, during the daily interactions with students and texts.

Multiple Collaborations

Our collaboration emerged spontaneously from the shared experiences, readings, questions, and discussions in graduate classrooms. Although our meetings have no formal sanction and fulfill no university degree requirements, our group did emerge out of, and in response to, an institutionalized setting. Thus, our group represents the formalized and shared backgrounds provided by graduate studies as well as the relatively unstructured environment of a collective freely chosen and pursued. We do have the advantage of shared knowledges about the coursework and texts and interactions of graduate study, as well as classroom teaching experiences.

However, the obstacles that served as impetus for the formation and continuation of our group are similar to those expressed by countless teachers, preservice teachers, administrators, supervisors, mentors, parents, and researchers in a variety of educational settings. These obstacles, expressed in our work as often-felt points of dissonance or as discrepancies or dissatisfactions in our daily lives as educators, reflect the situations and structures that confront us all.

Our chosen collaboration does not obliterate those obstacles but rather provides a clearing in which we can work to identify and grapple with them; our lack of institutionalized pressures or expectations allows us to step away from the routines and taken-for-granted arrangements of schools long enough to view our points of dissonance and our various discrepancies from different angles and from others' perspectives. Also, the fact that we all work in different settings relieves us of the pressures of creating immediate solutions to site-specific problems. Unlike many school-based collaborative projects, which emerge as problem-solving groups whose expectations often include end-product-like solutions and swift deliberation, our collaborative group feels no urge to reach premature closure nor to develop definitive answers to our constantly forming questions. Instead, we are able to focus upon our unique individual situations and concerns without pressure to reach consensus in our suggestions, reflections, or discussions. As Kevin noted, "our group provides a place to uncover what's really going on in our daily lives."

Our work together does not allow us, however, to conceive of our collaboration as a hiding place from the obstacles that we are addressing. Rather, as Cheryl said, our meetings are "a lifeline," signifying the necessary connection between our discussions and the actions that we take in our classrooms and offices. At the same time, given the lack of pressure to produce discernible end-results or products of our collaboration, we are aware that we may be slow in acting upon the discrepancies that our reflections have revealed thus far. One danger we have acknowledged is that we might remain in the comfort of the collaborative support without taking our emerging understandings into forms of action.

We also realize, through our own attempts to translate the forms and intentions of our collaboration into the contexts in which we work, that collaborative research groups often must function within formal or institutionalized contexts, such as in-service workshops or preservice practicums. The boundaries imposed by such structuring incorporate some of the very obstacles with which we have been wrestling, including elements of performance evaluation, of expert or leader-imposed research agendas and procedures, of subtle inequities in whose voices are raised and heard in the collaborative process, of the unspoken expectation for an end product.

Beth, in her role as district evaluator, continues, as we all do, to confront those obstacles in her work. She had noted, in our May 15, 1988, meeting, that she still feared distortions of the kind of collaborative interactions and research that we attempted:

> Our meetings and writings provide a moment of self for me. They allow me to step away and to recognize the system that I'm working in. When I'm there, it's so easy to get caught up in it. Here, even though we know that our work is part of being in the mess, at least I can get a handle on the organizational structure that still makes me feel like I have to get it right. Right now, all I can see are committees as a way to meet within the system. And as soon as you say "committee," people start to wonder about the agenda. I'm afraid that organized versions of what we do will never be able to be as free-floating and emergent as we are. My need for this group is a place to fight the system so that I don't get submerged, don't lose sight of me and of the bigger issues.

Beth, in her ongoing attempts to resist the distortions of our intentions that institutionalized collaboration might spawn, captures several of the dilemmas that we and others ponder. In our group, we share assumptions that our forms of collaborative inquiry do cast teachers as active contributors and creators in the processes of examining and improving not only their own practices but also the conditions and relationships that surround those practices. We agree that,

> teacher empowerment does not require the development of group process or leadership skills. Teachers are informed, concerned, and mature citizens. . . . [In] an environment that invites exchange, collegiality, self-esteem, teachers are confident, generous, and creative. Provided with the conditions that permit them to work together and to address the real issues that face them and their students, teachers can and do change schools (Grumet 1989, 24).

At the same time, we also have realized that quite often we will *not* be provided with those conditions that will foster the kinds of collaboration and collegiality that we are sharing within our group. In attempting to create those kinds of spaces within settings that do not foster or nourish such interactions, we now understand that our attempts at action, at creation, may be met with misunderstandings or rejections. As we try, without coercion or narrow versions of only one acceptable way, to overcome real obstacles in complex and often difficult situations, we also try to be mindful of Welch's (1985) warning that "it is possible that our thought and our action share in the perpetuation of as yet unrecognized forms of oppression" (85–86).

To be mindful of that warning implies that collaborative associations need to be of long duration in order to take into account the complex constraints of those who want to uncover "as yet unrecognized forms of oppression." As clearly demonstrated in our work together thus far, the layers of internalized assumptions and expectations with which we grapple are oppressively thick. Our attempts to uncover those layers of expectations for ourselves as teachers, to see ways in which expectations have been constructed through the intersections of external and internal forces in our lives, to examine effects of our acceptances of those as givens, and to work to change those taken-for-granted assumptions, continue to be

153

difficult and meandering. Beth's worry that such work might be condensed into a series of predetermined goal-driven committee meetings or in-service workshops reflects the concerns of many who wish to honor the strengths that collaborative inquiry might provide but who work in settings where collaboration now means mere participation rather than "equitable and consensual inquiry" (Oakes, Hare, and Sirotnik 1986).

Beth's worries also point to conceptions of collaboration that in no way attempt to address the issues of imposition and oppression that engage us. For those who are concerned with "effectiveness" and "reform" but who do not wish to examine the underlying assumptions that continue to place teachers in a deficit position within those movements, Marjorie's comments from an April 2, 1989, meeting might not be welcomed:

> What I'm realizing is that how we see our own constraints as individual teachers, educators, does reflect the hierarchical structures that most of us see no way of changing. When I think of our picnic, when we started this whole thing, I remember that I was almost in tears at that picnic because I could only see the invitation as an either–or. I thought that, if I joined this teacher-researcher group, I'd have to give up being a state mentor. I just couldn't see doing both because they just didn't fit together. I couldn't see how doing the mentor work could be empowering for anyone. It's only this far down the line that I can see that teachers posing their own problems and asking their own questions is a form of action and empowerment that we have been working to understand and to effect.

Given the swelling number of collaborative projects that are emerging as a result of the press for teachers' professional development, another concern that emerges from our work, then, is the possible underlying dichotomy of intent to which Marjorie alludes. Many conceive of collaboration as a way in which teachers can work together to improve their teaching practices. While that emphasis certainly has emerged as part of our collaborative inquiry, it also has the potential to be posited as the *only* goal of collaboration. As such, that emphasis has the potential to obscure the possibilities of teacher-centered inquiry that also focuses on uncovering forms of oppression and imposition within school settings. Marjorie originally saw our potential work as a form of direct opposition to the prescribed forms of mentoring in which she would be participating and to her accustomed role of teacher, not researcher; that she feared she would have to make a choice between the two orientations indicates the degree to which many educators might view our collaborative group's goals and processes as outside the realm of possibility or desirability within existing school structures:

> What forms of organizational life encourage teacher educators, teachers, and pre-service teachers to become open to and empowered by what is initially perceived as threatening and negative? . . . Critical consciousness cannot be mandated. . . . One must also be prepared to challenge traditional power relationships between teacher educators, teachers, and future teachers. Thus, the problem is not only one of educating the education student, but also of educating the educator. (Britzman 1988, 93)

We continue to question, as part of our collaborative inquiry. Is it possible to create preservice and in-service contexts in which teachers can set the agenda for the forms and purposes of their inquiry? How might we encourage forms of our collaborative inquiry within contexts that ordinarily have predetermined agendas for intent and content? Is it possible to envision forms of collaboration within and across institutions among peers, whether they be teachers working with teachers, with administrators, with student teachers, with university or community members, in which each is involved in processes and content that might uncover the taken-for-granted, the submerged inequalities that ultimately prevent reform and improvement in our schools? How might we create possibilities for empowerment through the ways we confront those submerged and habitual and often inequitable relationships? How can we encourage administrative, peer, and community support for the lengthy investigations that such goals entail? For,

> changing fundamental beliefs and ideas involves recognizing the shape of the conscious and unconscious ideas we already have, including elements that are oppressive both to ourselves and others. It involves understanding how we came to have the ideas we have. It also involves understanding what interests might be served by the views we have come to take for granted. (Berlak 1989, 18)

Given our three-year collaboration, our commitment to ongoing pursuit of these questions and to asking new questions spawned by these, we now see the necessity of extended forms of collaborative inquiry. We do understand more deeply than before that "change . . . is not a simple escape from constraint to liberation" (Martin and Mohanty 1986, 201).

Thus, these questions come from our long-term interaction and now frame our examination of current versions of educational collaboration, even as we attempt to participate in their various forms in our individual educational settings. We think that questions such as these also must inform the work of staff developers and university faculty, in particular, as these individuals often are the ones who formulate, conduct, and evaluate teacher preparation and in-service programs.

However, the role of teachers as initiators of such collaborative programs is now becoming more possible. Wigginton (1989), for example, who with students in his English classes researched and created the *Foxfire* books and magazines, offers a compelling account of the formation of networks of teachers who have participated in courses that address the philosophy and teaching activities undergirding student-produced versions of cultural journalism. These networks across the United States provide support and a meeting place for teachers who wish to continue in the dialogue begun in their original coursework. As Wigginton notes, in order to avoid superficial or distorted versions of the original principles that guide this work, teachers must continually engage in critical self-examination of their theory and practice. The networks support Wigginton's contention that when several teachers get together, "they themselves represent the answers to all their dilemmas" (39).

Although the *Foxfire* networks are representative of several forms of collaborative teacher-centered groups that are functioning across the country,[1] many teachers still must respond to the mandates of district or state versions of collaboration, where the emphasis often is on development of teachers' "skills" as a means of school improvement. Part of our emphasis on our emerging questions about collaboration is an attempt to call attention to the deficit model of teachers' knowledge that still accompanies such versions of collaboration and to the detrimental effects of such models on teachers' perceptions of their own abilities and possibilities:

> The lack of a sufficient number of forums in which teachers carry on in-depth conversations over long periods of time perpetuates the view that

teachers' knowledge has little to contribute to further understanding in the field. Teachers, who most frequently experience their peers either in informal settings or in staff development programs in which their usual role is audience, have few opportunities to see the more reflective, knowledgeable side of their colleagues. They conclude, reasonably but erroneously, that teachers as a group are not very impressive and have little to contribute to the formation of educational theory or the solution of educational problems. (Evans, Stubbs, Frechette, Neely, and Warner 1987, 4)

Our questions also raise examples of ways in which we all, at one time or another, have attempted to resist enforced collegiality by withdrawing, like Katherine with her earphones and darkened library, into daily routines and patterns of isolation that serve as effective personal conservation strategies (Flinders 1988) against mandated forms of collaboration that function to correct teachers' "deficiencies."

For example, Smith (1987) describes elements of a collaborative school in terms that reinforce notions of teachers' professional knowledge as a set of skills that need to be improved in order for school improvement to take place:

Collaboration depends on the voluntary effort of educators to improve their schools and their own skills through teamwork. . . . Although a host of other benefits may be expected to derive from collaboration—staff harmony, mutual respect between teachers and administrators, and a professional work environment for teachers—its primary rationale is instructional effectiveness. Its most important dynamic comes from teachers' working together to improve their teaching. (5)

In a similar vein, Glatthorn (1987) discusses cooperative professional development as a form of peer-oriented systems, and suggests ways in which these forms might be systematized in order to strengthen teachers' practice. In each of his delineations, including professional dialogue, curriculum development, peer supervision, peer coaching, and action research, Glatthorn reinforces the hierarchical arrangements under which such peer-oriented systems may take place:

There is strong leadership at the school level: the principal takes leadership in fostering norms of collegiality, in modeling collaboration and cooperation, and by rewarding teacher cooperation. . . . Under the leadership of their principal, each school's faculty members review the guidelines and analyze

157

the various collaborative options. . . . Those guidelines specify such matters as: which program options may be offered at the school level; which teachers will be eligible to participate in the cooperative programs; how schools may provide time for the cooperative programs; how the programs may be evaluated; how the programs will be administered and coordinated at the district level. (34–35)

Lieberman (1986), although not explicitly challenging bureaucratic and positivist conceptions of school improvement, comes closer to the intent and concerns of our collaborative group when she discusses the variations of collaborative work and the understandings needed to sustain such activity:

Contexts, needs, talents, and commitments differ, but one thing appears to be constant: schools cannot improve without people working together. . . . None of us, no matter what our position, has the answers to the complex problems we face. The more people work together, the more we have the possibility of better understanding these complex problems and acting on them in an atmosphere of trust and mutual respect. We need to understand not only the variety of collaborative activities and arrangements, but what people get from these relationships and what it takes to sustain them. (6)

We continue to concentrate, in our group, not only on what we get from these relationships but also on what we can do to share the support and acceptance as well as the modes of inquiry that have enabled us to sustain our meetings and dialogues. We know that the issues of imposition and control that are embedded in the more bureaucratic and positivist conceptions of collaboration are issues that we must constantly face in our own interactions; at the same time, we also believe that this very focus has enabled us to continue together, even though each of us, at various times, has had qualms about being able to remain in the group or to translate the nature and forms of our work into daily educational settings.

Oakes, Hare, and Sirotnik (1986), in their focus on possible forms of collaboration between university researchers and classroom teachers, argue for more than mere participation as one criterion for collaboration. In doing so, they acknowledge the constant threat of unconscious impositions upon participants' conceptions of the collaborative process:

The teachers, probably conditioned by their experiences of being relatively powerless in the hierarchical structure of schooling, erred in the direction of silence. They did not risk confronting the entire team with their feelings of being unsupported until long after damage was done. The researchers erred in the direction of arrogance. Concerned about not imposing their values as to what constitutes good lessons, the research staff imposed instead their view of what constitutes collaborative "leadership." (555)

Welch's warning about participating in unidentified forms of oppression resonates here. Furthermore, in this example, we are reminded that we cannot divest ourselves of those vestiges of authority that strike us as unproductive simply by ignoring the institutional arrangements that, although here created in the name of collaboration, unequally empower the participants (Brodkey 1989).

Oakes, Hare, and Sirotnik's attempts to make explicit the difficulties embedded within notions of collaborative inquiry are echoed in Campbell's (1988) description of the role dilemmas and contradictions experienced among a group of classroom teachers and university researchers involved in a staff development project that engaged participants in reflection and dialogue grounded in respect for teachers' knowledge. Well into the project, in which the university researchers were conducting research on this supposedly teacher-determined staff development process, the university researchers were confronted with the teachers' suspicions of a "hidden agenda" for the focus on reading research; this area was a major interest for several of the university researchers but not for several of the teachers in the project. Campbell discusses the difficulties that the teachers' suspicions revealed:

Forswearing an interventionist intent merely leaves open the possibility of intervening by default, unintentionally but with no less danger precisely because the intervention is obscured from the researcher's view, if not the practitioner's. I have in mind here the fact that decisions about what *is* studied leave other things *unstudied,* thus leaving alternative paths for improving educational practice unexplored. The more insidious possibility is that the mystique of expertise that researchers and their findings often convey, even if unintentionally, can reinforce received and privileged views, thereby inhibiting practitioners from taking control of their professional lives. (117)

Campbell's point is similar to Harding's (1987): the questions that are asked, and, more important, the questions that are not asked, are as determinative of the adequacy of our total picture as are any

159

answers that we might discover. One strength that we have discovered in the duration and consistency of our own meetings is the extended opportunity for the heretofore unasked questions to emerge. In a sense, our long-term collaboration has enabled us "to swing into view sides and facets that are normally turned away and unseen" (de Beaugrande 1988, 258).

Thus, Katherine's query, "would we still meet if Janet were not involved in this group," for example, allowed us to explore questions that had to do with individual as well as collective assumptions that we all were making about our meetings, dialogues, writing, and research, and about our roles within each of those forms and relationships. These explorations might normally have remained "turned away and unseen," had we not persisted in exploring our own reasons for wanting to collaborate and to research in ways that interrupt taken-for-granted educational perspectives and relationships.

The examination of possible impositions, assumptions, and unequal power relationships within collaborative frameworks points to the difficulty in developing modes of collaborative inquiry that do not embody covert replications of existing inequitable relationships between teachers and university researchers or administrators or students. Although these examinations often are painful for us, we have come to believe that attempts to form collaborative communities of educators are futile unless such examinations become a part of the very collaborative process itself.

Thus we conceive the purposes of collaboration to include examinations of ourselves, of the possibilities of changing our relationships and schooling systems which often reflect inequitable and oppressive conditions in the world outside our classrooms, and of the possible processes of collaboration. These purposes do not negate the more narrow and site-specific problems of curriculum and instruction that motivate many forms of collaborative investigation or staff development. Rather, they add to those foci the possibilities of disrupting established meanings, values, and power relations embedded in issues of curriculum and instruction and collaboration; by examining the origins of those established meanings, values, and power relations, and whose interests they support, and how these interests maintain their sovereignty, we may be able to discern where they are susceptible to change (Weedon 1987).

160

For members of our collaborative research group, the emphasis in our work continues to be on ways in which we first can see and then begin to disrupt those established patterns of meaning and power relationships. We find that we have to focus on aspects of our daily lives in order to concretize the possibilities of collaborating for change in our schools. One of our challenges, confronted daily in our classrooms, offices, in-service workshops, and student teaching seminars, is

> to become capable of a sustained encounter with currently oppressive formations and power relations that refuse to be theorized away or fully transcended in a utopian resolution—and to enter into the encounter in a way that owns up to [our] own implications in those formations and [is] capable of changing [our] own relation to and investments in those formations. (Ellsworth 1989, 308)

As we attempt to own up to our own participation in such formations, we are convinced that the positive support and various perspectives that inform our collaboration are necessary components if we are to attempt changes in ourselves and in our schools. Even though we acknowledge that we always are "simultaneously a part of several discourses, several communities, . . . already committed to a number of conflicting beliefs and practices" (Harris 1989, 19), we also believe in the possibilities of building what Harris calls "communities without consensus." We are striving to create spaces for dialogue and human action that open the way to communities

> marked by an articulate public—no longer silenced, no longer mystified, . . . [who] could pursue themselves as distinctive beings *because* they were participants in ongoing conversation, because they were aware of social insufficiencies, because they were committed to transform. (Greene 1990, 75)

To participate in ongoing conversation does not mean that we in our collaborative group necessarily reach consensus. It does mean, however, that we must attempt to acknowledge the ways in which our work together is framed by the prevailing educational discourses of our institutional settings:

> There is no privileged position from which one can speak without one's own discourse being itself put into question. However, it is precisely through the willingness to undertake a critical examination of the assumptions underlying our own discourse that we may acquire the means to make

choices about how to speak, and write, and teach in ways that move toward the kind of social arrangements we desire. (Elbaz and Elbaz 1989, 128)

Thus, we also must attempt to see ways in which our conceptions of collaboration, of research, of teaching and learning are constantly open to redefinition. The teacher-as-researcher orientation to our collaborative inquiries continues to challenge us to view and review our work together as well as our work in schools in ways that allow us to create those redefinitions.

Multiple Researchers

In arguing that personal history is good research, Krall (1988) points to aspects of our collaborative inquiry that have provided impetus for us to view, review, and redefine. Krall explicates her conception of good research:

> By "good" I mean that it should bring deeper meaning into our daily lives without controlling the lives of others. It should not reduce the complexities of human interaction and learning to simple formulas but rather should elaborate and accentuate their richness. As a result of our research, we should become more consciously intentional of our actions and more thoughtful and reflective of their consequences. (474)

Within our collaborative group, we try to see our work together, our writing and discussions and debates, as forms of good research. As we entered into our third year, I think our collaborative group began to view our developing and multiple narratives as research both upon our individual personal histories and upon our evolving conceptions of our possibilities as educators. As such, our collaborative research remains focused on our interactive and relational processes as well as on our attempts to address the interplay of shifting consciousnesses, agencies, and outside social forces involved in our collaborative attempts.

These perspectives link our work to the teacher-as-researcher orientations that emphasize elements of emancipatory action research, in which practitioners attempt "to search out not only interpretive meanings that educational actions have for them but to organize actions to overcome constraints on action" (McKernan

1988, 183). Such research involves the simultaneous organization of a self-reflective community:

> Emancipatory action research includes the impulses and forms of practical action research but extends them into a collaborative context. The critical impulse of emancipatory action research towards the transformation of educational institutions is expressed not only in individual critical thinking but in the common critical enterprise of changing selves in order to change the institutions those selves generate through their joint practices of communication, decision-making, work and social action. (Carr and Kemmis 1986, 204)

Action research in education, grounded in the early work of Lewin in sociology, was initially developed most notably by Stenhouse in Great Britain;[2] he insisted that the professional contexts of teachers, their classrooms, be the settings in which educational research took place, and that,

> the theory or insight created in collaboration by professional researchers and professional teachers is always provisional, always to be tested and modified by professional practice. The teacher who founds his practice of teaching upon research must adopt a research stance to his own practice: it must be provisional and exploratory. (Stenhouse 1985, 126)

Although promoting the teacher as central in educational research, the work of Stenhouse did not satisfy all the criteria deemed necessary by emancipatory action researchers, in that his emphasis on teacher-as-researcher remained individualistic and centered in the practical. In practical action research, teachers monitor their own educational practices with the immediate goal of developing their practical judgment as individuals. Those judgments are enacted in classrooms; thus, an overarching goal of practical action research is

> deliberate, group or personally owned and conducted, solution-oriented investigation. . . . Whenever people decide to learn, they undertake research. If teachers wish deliberately to learn about their teaching, they must research. If children wish to learn about electricity, they must research. Learning is defined as understanding in such a way that one can say it in one's own words and be understood, or do it and be effective. (Boomer 1987, 8)

Stenhouse particularly advocated the case study of one unit, whether an individual classroom, or student, or teacher, as the means by which researchers could study teachers' particular situations; teachers could then utilize case studies as comparative contexts in which to judge their own situations, and to "say it" in their own words.

> In justifying the contribution of case study research to the professional development of teachers, Stenhouse argued that educational theory must be tested by how well it fits with the realities of experience in schools and classrooms. Case studies provide evidence of such realities and give practitioners a way to test theory. They constitute, in a sense, a bridge between the academic researcher, who constructs theory from a range of experiences from which he or she is distanced, and the practitioners themselves, whose experience is, by comparison, limited but compensated by detail, depth, and continuity. Case study research, as Stenhouse tried to develop it, offers both a way of grounding inquiry in the experience of teachers and pupils and a means of promoting dialogue about practice. (Rudduck 1988, 39)

As conceptualized in these descriptions of the form and purpose of practical action research, subtle distinctions still remain between academic researchers and classroom teachers. The teacher could function as a focus of research and development in this conceptualization, but still sometimes remain as consumer, critiquer, and tester of others' research.

Many versions of practical action research do involve teachers as active participants in their own classroom research (Allen, Combs, Hendricks, Nash, and Wilson 1988; Bissex and Bullock 1987; Goswami and Stillman 1987; Gregory 1988; Hitchcock and Hughes 1989), as well as in the examination of the forms of research that they choose. In developing a guide for classroom teacher-researchers, Mohr and MacLean (1987), although primarily interested in research on the teaching of writing, point to the necessity of examining conceptions and approaches within various research paradigms as an essential element within all teacher-researcher activity. By discussing underlying assumptions that accompany particular research frameworks, and by sharing examples of teachers' processes of debate and choice among those frameworks, Mohr and MacLean's guide does accent the active role of teachers in deciding not only their research questions but also in examining the epistemological assumptions that will frame their research approaches.

164

Case studies continue to predominate as teachers' preferred orientation in research, especially on writing; but here, as conceptualized by Mohr, MacLean and others, and as detailed throughout this narrative, case studies are conceived, developed, and analyzed by classroom teachers in response to their own questions about their classrooms. Rather than testing the theories emanating from outside researchers' case studies, teacher-researchers who actively participate in posing their research questions and conducting research processes are challenging some subtle hierarchical versions of practical action research.

Emancipatory action researchers, however, argue that these activities are not sufficient for challenging the taken-for-granted discourses and structures which form and frame teaching and research processes. In emancipatory action research,

> the practitioner group takes joint responsibility for the development of practice, understandings, and situations, and sees these as socially constructed in the interactive processes of educational life. It does not treat teacher responsibility for classroom interaction as an individual matter, but, on the contrary, takes the view that the character of classroom interaction is also a matter for school determination and decision making. (Carr and Kemmis 1986, 203)

We continue, in our collaborative teacher-researcher stance, to investigate the socially constructed aspects of our personal experiences and conceptions of our practice as teacher, counselor, or administrator; we still struggle, however, with ways in which to extend those investigations beyond the boundaries of our group meetings and classrooms and offices into the larger arenas "of school determination and decision making."

Thus, what remains important in Stenhouse's work for our collaborative group is the insistence upon the provisional and exploratory nature of the research process itself as well as upon the contextualized world of the classroom as focus for teacher-researchers. These perspectives are linked to our evolving understandings of the important role of personal history in the enactments of what Krall (1988) defines as "good research." Many of our group's goals do center on our attempts to research and to understand the ways in which our work as teachers is formed both by specific social and historical conditions and by our potentials to act upon those conditions. We continue to uncover layers of assumptions that illuminate how

> our personal and cultural (including school) experiences have converged to convey the taken-for-grantedness of particular patterns of resolution. By inquiring into the origins of particular patterns or preferences, a teacher may come to see, for example, how the almost exclusive emphasis on public knowledge, knowledge as content, and teacher control of standards in her own school experiences, made it nearly inevitable that she would replicate this pattern in her own teaching. (Berlak and Berlak 1987, 176)

At the same time, we have struggled to extend our research on the origins and manifestations of patterns in our daily educators' lives into research that also allows us to "learn to attend to the politics of what we do and do not do at a practical level, . . . and to look closely at our own practice in terms of how we contribute to dominance in spite of our liberatory intents" (Lather 1989a, 6–8). However, in order to attempt such research, we have found that we must detail our emerging understandings of these dimensions of our practice in our own voices and within the spaces and situations that we encounter daily.

Thus we also share McKernan's (1988) concern about the ways in which the theoretical scaffolding of critical action research has not been developed by, and grounded in, the language and interpretive categories of practitioners. That concern, in fact, was part of the impetus of my original invitation to members of our group, and remains central to our developing rationale for collaborative forms of teacher-centered inquiry.

We agree that a form of collaborative action research is needed involving emancipation-oriented curriculum theorists and practitioners sympathetic with their views. However, we also agree that,

> emancipation-oriented theorists and practitioners must answer many questions. How can teachers avoid creating self-fulfilling prophesies about students from different ethnic groups, yet still accomodate and value ethnic diversity? . . . Children from primarily oral cultures, for instance, will likely be less proficient with written language when they enter school. The difference is likely to be real, not simply a product of the teacher's imagination, and teachers need strategies to confront these differences in ways that will not perpetuate existing inequalities. Similarly, how can principals or superintendents sympathetic with emancipation-oriented analyses of education behave on a day-to-day basis? (Donmoyer 1989, 268–269)

Questions such as these highlight collaborative research possibilities, without denying the provisional and exploratory nature of the researching process itself, and while acknowledging the contextualized needs and concerns of educators who must confront these issues on a daily basis.

Hopkins (1987) describes teacher research as a process of teachers' being reflective and critical about, and consequently taking more control over, their professional lives. In that description, Hopkins, like McKernan, points to the necessary grounding of such research in the daily situations and languages of teachers themselves. At the same time, he alludes to the possibilities that can emerge within practitioner-initiated and practitioner-voiced inquiries that are linked to the intent of critical action research:

> By virtue of being a teacher researcher . . . , one is inevitably making a political statement. Political in the sense that the individual is supporting a method of teaching that is emancipatory and runs counter to the normative order. . . . I do not claim that merely by becoming a teacher researcher the whole gamut of socio-political ills will be remedied, but I do believe that within the concept lies the potential for transformation. (Hopkins 1987, 126)

Hopkins links the processes and purposes of teaching and research in ways that reinforce reasons for our attempting to become teacher-researchers. As we work to act in ways congruent with our understandings of the relationships of theory and practice, reflection and action, teaching and research, we have become aware of our own possibilities. In turn, this awareness enables us to see the "potential for transformation," not only for ourselves but also for the educational communities in which we work. This awareness of possibilities has compelled each of us to "become vocal," as Katherine called it. As part of our developing confidence in our own voices and in our resulting willingness to speak and to question, we understand that we are acting and speaking and researching in ways that could challenge the taken-for-granted and that run "counter to the normative order."

Thus, we all are becoming more comfortable in talking about both our individual and collaborative work as research. And we can start using the languages of our classrooms and counseling offices and district meeting rooms as one way to disrupt the controlling and predictive forms and intentions of the prevailing discourse in educational research.

However, our particular forms of collaboration in teacher research do not fit easily into the categories described here. In part, this is because we are still struggling to understand how to conduct forms of research that, by focusing on the social relations of research itself, produce a collaborative analysis that does not impose one researcher's understanding of reality, that does not, via a privileged position and theoretical presuppositions, say what things mean (Gitlin, Siegel, and Boru 1988). The narrative journeys shared in this book exemplify one attempt to grapple with these emerging forms of research; by juxtaposing the verbal and written dialogues of all the group members, as well as by calling attention to our varied points of dissonance and the questions that emerge and reemerge in our explorations, each member shares in the formation and reformulation of this text and of our continuing processes of collaboration and research.

By speaking and questioning in our own voices, rather than in the voices of outside researchers and theoreticians, each of us also has been able to analyze some of the connections and interplay among personal and social forces that influence our practice. We now are asking difficult questions of one another in our meetings and in our dialogue journals. In accepting the challenge that, in order to interrupt existing power relations, "our best examples must be ourselves" (Van Maanen 1988, xv), questions have become our way of interrupting our own taken-for-granted assumptions about teaching, research, and curriculum. Our continuing challenge now is to ask questions of ourselves as well as of those with whom we work and interact in schools, knowing that the questions and our own voices will be constantly emerging and changing. Thus we now at least understand that, although we often would like to find definitive answers, the crux of our work lies within the constant raising of questions in spaces and in voices that, although complex and differing and internally changing, are our own.

Multiple Voices

As our collaborative inquiry continues, and as we experience our versions of research and collaboration in ever-changing ways, we also have come see and hear ourselves in differing forms and contexts. This points to the ways in which our voices, although perhaps louder now than when we began our association, are *not* now fixed, unified, coherent, undivided representations of a whole and conscious self (Morton and Zavarzadeh 1989). Rather, we now, more than when we began, hear that our voices express multiple and often contradictory possibilities for ourselves. We continue to look for and try to create spaces in which the experiences of our daily lives as educators can be articulated in their multiplicities:

> In practice this always implies a struggle—a struggle over assigned meaning, a struggle over discourse as the expression of both form and content, a struggle over interpretation of experience, and a struggle over "self." . . . It is a struggle that makes possible new knowledge that expands beyond individual experience and hence redefines our identities and the real possibilities we see in the daily conditions of our lives. . . . It is the struggle through which new knowledge, identities, and possibilities are introduced that may lead to the alteration simultaneously of circumstances and selves. (Lewis and Simon 1986, 469)

As we attempt to create space for uncertainty, dialogue, and new possibilities in ourselves, in our collaborative research and in our classrooms and offices, we are trying to be aware of the questions that must accompany the creation of such space and the acknowledgement of the partial and often contradictory nature of our own and others' voices:

> Whose voices are heard? Whose are silenced and why? What are the power relations that open or close access to conversations, whether spoken or written? . . . What conditions must be obtained for those who have been silenced to feel safe in dialogue? . . . What prior agreements need to be established to ensure a place where each person can speak her or his own mind and heart? What does a teacher need to know, feel, experience, in order to provide mutuality and reciprocity among diverse voices? (Kohli 1989, 105–106)

Questions such as these inform the evolving forms of our collaboration and point to the provisional and fluid nature of both our research processes and our modes of collaborative inquiry. They inform our group's interactions as well as our actions within our individual settings.

For example, I had suggested, even during that picnic lunch where I made the invitation to begin these explorations, that we try dialogue journal writing as one way in which to explore the

169

interactive aspects of our collaborative endeavors. As our narratives throughout this book suggest, that form of journal writing did not become comfortable for Katherine until well into our second year of work. Even then, as she noted, the writing came in surges, often followed by weeks in which Katherine did not write at all. Others in the group found the dialogue journal writing to be a constant space in which to push through points of dissonance or to explore, in depth, those stings restimulated throughout our collaboration.

At our meeting of September 25, 1988, Beth noted that she really thought that we could begin to "share the dialogue journal writing in more ways with one another." Some group members had exchanged letters throughout our work thus far, as another form of dialogue, and all of us had had many conversations outside our scheduled meeting times; now all agreed that they felt comfortable in sharing their more formal dialogue journal writing with one another as well as with me. When I asked what had precipitated their willingness, as we moved into our third year together, to exchange journals with one another, Marjorie replied:

> I think that, as we discussed the evolving chapters of this book and gave you suggestions and choices of emphasis in journal entries and other feedback, and as I read what was emerging in each of the chapters, based on all our discussions and suggestions to you, I really could see how much each of our journals enlarged upon what we discussed and wrangled about in our meetings. As much as I feel that I know the struggles of each of us from our meetings and long-term interactions, I now feel, when I read all those journal entries, a bigger dimension to what we are doing. I feel even closer and more connected to the struggles that we all share.

Beth replied:

> Yes, the writing and now the reading about us has given us another layer to look through, to see what we've done and where we want to go. The "carton of knowledge" episode, for example, was so powerful in retrospect, and in seeing all the extensions that have come from that, I think that we all can go even deeper now.

When we began our collaboration, and as we attempted to respond to one another across the limitations of our daily lives, members of the group often would mail their journal entries to me as well as bring their journals to our meeting; I, in turn, would write back, often in letter form, and would attempt to respond to individual's questions and musings, as well as to share my own concerns and reflections that resulted from our exchanges and from the unfolding events and issues of our work. Often, our journal entries to one another overlapped, not only temporally, but also in focus. Sometimes these overlappings took the form of letters crossing in the mail; as we became familiar with one another's points of dissonance and layers of assumptions, our writing to one another also overlapped by pointing to the similarities and differences among our responses to these recurring themes.

As a result of this discussion, however, the group will begin to shift the ways in which we handle the dialogue journal writing. Although we cannot say, at this point, into what new patterns our exchanges might fall, we are aware of the changing nature and functions of our dialogue journal writing. We now see the extent to which the group members' interest in expanding our interaction also reflects possible new directions and expression of our work together.

As we move into new patterns of written dialogue with one another, we will add a variety of questioning and responding voices to our individual concerns and research pursuits. Our extended and expansive journal dialogues could serve to emphasize the complex, intertwined, and evolving situations in which we write and talk with one another, as well as our similar and different responses to those situations. We could simultaneously begin to explore how our collective dialogue journal writing might constitute experiences that could enable us "to provide mutuality and reciprocity among diverse voices" (Kohli 1989). Given our growing awareness of the multiplicity of voices within each of us, our expanded forms of dialogue journal writing also might enable each of us to hear those multiplicities, not only in our voices but also in those of the others in our group. Given the feelings of safety and acceptance that our collaboration has created, such a chorus of voices could allow us to acknowledge our own individual partiality and limitations "in order to be open to the multiplicity, the complexity, and value of another" (Newton and Hoffman 1988, 9).

We see this possibility as the foremost reason for encouraging others to consider the forms and intentions of our collaborative inquiry, for we are convinced that our shared encounters have enabled us to see and hear and act differently in the larger arenas in which we conduct our educational lives. We still struggle with the seemingly small gestures that, for us, constitute what we mean by acting "differently." Marjorie questioned, in our meeting of April 30, 1989, how she might, in her supervisory role as mentor, write encouraging notes to teachers without sounding condescending and patronizing. How might she carry out her administrative role without reinforcing the dependent and subjugated roles for teachers who looked to her for approval and guidance? How can we "interrupt these teachers' agendas," as Marjorie put it, without undermining these teachers' confidence in themselves or her?

Beth keeps pointing out to us that we all made a conscious choice to interrupt our professional and personal agendas, so to speak, in order to join this collaborative group. When there is "very little room for conversation" and constant pressure for closure, as Beth noted in that April meeting, how can we infuse our work with the possibilities for choice, for transformation?

Questions such as these represent the seemingly small interrupting gestures that we now make in our separate educational settings. Though perhaps subtle in observable detail, we know that our willingness to raise questions, to challenge the habitual responses of ourselves and others, signifies our moving beyond the safety of our collaboration and into the worlds where we teach, administer and counsel.

For it is within the activities of our daily lives, in the gatherings in the hallways and classrooms and offices and counseling cubicles of school buildings where our forms of emancipatory research and pedagogy must take place. In these small spaces, teachers, students, administrators, counselors, parents will continue the dialogues that began in classes, or in the department meetings, or over coffee after the Parents' Night presentations, or in the early morning hours of bus-duty, or even at a picnic lunch that became a celebration of both endings and beginnings.

Within these daily spaces, clearings forged in the midst of permission slips and mandated curriculum and computer print-outs of test scores, educators do recognize that the fissures of teaching and research, theory and practice, public and private, are artificial distinctions that separate us from ourselves and from the relationships in which knowledges about self and about our worlds are generated.

In the sharing of our stories, then, we know that others will have different versions and tales to tell. Our hope is that, through the sharing of our interactions and through the presentation of possible alternatives represented in our particular approaches to our work, others will want to gather together and to begin.

NOTES

Chapter Two: Creating Spaces

1. In New York State, the Board of Cooperative Educational Services (BOCES) enables school districts to contribute money for shared services, which BOCES then arranges for and provides. These services, such as special or vocational education and teacher in-service programs, often are too costly for school districts separately to offer on an individual or single-unit basis.

Chapter Four: Points of Dissonance

1. I discuss this separation in detail in Chapter Six. A number of researchers have explored the effects of teacher separation from the interactive aspects of theory and research creation. McNeil (1986) describes "defensive teaching" as a series of strategies that teachers employ to maintain their own "authorities and efficiencies," strategies that Apple (1986) and McNeil claim ultimately contribute to teachers' "deskilling." As teachers focus on their particular subject matter and become caught up in the presentation of "facts" that represent "knowledge," teachers have no time or incentives to research, with their students, their constructions of or their relationships to that knowledge.

   Berlak (1988) writes of these separations of teaching and research from a teacher's perspective, as she attempts to struggle through the forms of imposition that teachers embody, even in their attempts to participate in liberating teaching and research practices.

   Lewis and Simon (1986) share research of themselves as graduate student and teacher who experience, quite differently, their study of the

175

relationships of language and power. Their work offers a profound example of the difficulties as well as the possible reciprocal relationships of teaching and research, of reflection and action, that can occur in classrooms.

2. The phrases "writing as a way of learning" and "writing as a way of knowing" characterize the writing process movement that originated as the Bay Area Writing Project in the United States in the early 1970s.

3. Moffett's program for "writing across the curriculum," for years only available in an underground, experimental version, is now published in revised form (1981) for elementary through college levels.

Chapter Five: Becoming Challengers

1. Various perspectives on the historical antecedents and contemporary manifestations of the "feminization of teaching" are part of a growing body of research within curriculum studies in particular, and within educational studies in general. Hoffman's (1981) historical account of the development of teaching into "women's 'true' profession" emphasizes the voices of women as they struggled, within the confines of social expectations and schooling structures, to create and to choose teaching as their vocation. Anyon's (1984) analysis focuses on the intersections of class and gender in these struggles, while my interviews with women teachers (Miller 1986) attempt to present women's voices as they grapple with the intersections of their personal and public lives. Grumet's account (1988a) of the development of a "pedagogy for patriarchy" emphasizes, more so than the analyses of Apple (1986), Goodman (1988), or Tabakin and Densmore (1986), the intentionality as well as the compromises and distortions that characterized women's lives as they made teaching into women's work. Laird (1988) and Pagano (1990) extend these issues to examine the difficulties inherent in conceptualizations of "feminist pedagogy."

Epilogue: "We're Not Done Yet"

1. Examples of teacher-initiated and -focused collaborative groups include The Educational Forum, now affiliated with the Harvard Teachers' Network, which meets to design, implement, and interpret teacher-conducted classroom investigations. Project START, or Student Teachers as Researching Teachers, is a teacher-preparation program, housed in the Graduate School of Education at the University of Pennsylvania; it emphasizes reflection and inquiry about teaching theory and practice. In addition to the usual combination of observing and gradually taking on teaching responsibilities, student teachers in Project START work collaboratively with their cooperating teachers on classroom research projects. The Institute for Democracy in Education, housed at Ohio University, serves as both a support and advocate for development of teachers' research and practice as exemplars of education for democratic empowerment. The National Council of Teachers of English, through its Research Foundation, funds a series of teacher-as-researcher grants each year; classroom teachers from any grade level may apply.

2. Kemmis and McTaggart (1982), Carr and Kemmis (1986), Hopkins (1987) and McKernan (1988) all offer excellent historical accounts of the origins, development, and processes of action research in educational settings. Attention also is given to the influence of action research perspectives developed in noneducation settings as well as to education projects developed in Great Britain, Australia, and the United States.

BIBLIOGRAPHY

Alcoff, L. 1988. Cultural feminism versus post-structuralism: The identity crisis in feminist theory. *Signs: Journal of Women in Culture and Society* 13: 405–436.

Allen, J., J. Combs, M. Hendricks, P. Nash, and S. Wilson. 1988. Studying change: Teachers who become researchers. *Language Arts* 65: 379–387.

Anyon, J. 1981. Social class and school knowledge. *Curriculum Inquiry* 11: 3–42.

———. 1984. Intersections of gender and class: Accomodation and resistance by working-class and affluent females to contradictory sex-role ideologies. *Journal of Education* 166: 25–48.

Apple, M. W. 1986. *Teachers and texts: A political economy of class and gender relations in education.* New York: Routledge and Kegan Paul.

Applebee, A. 1987. Musings . . . teachers and the process of research. *Research in the Teaching of English* 21: 5–7.

179

Ashton, P. T., and R. B. Webb. 1986. *Making a difference: Teachers' sense of efficacy and student achievement.* New York: Longman.

Atwell, N. 1987. Building a dining room table: Dialogue journals about reading. In *The journal book,* ed. T. Fulwiler, 157–170. Portsmouth, NH: Boynton/Cook Publishers.

Benhabib, S., and D. Cornell, eds. 1987. *Feminism as critique.* Minneapolis: University of Minnesota Press.

Berlak, A. 1988. Teaching for outrage and empathy in the liberal arts. Paper presented at Annual Meeting of American Educational Research Association, April, New Orleans.

———. 1989. Angles of vision on emancipatory pedagogy: Some "takes" on the first five weeks. Paper presented at Annual Meeting of American Educational Research Association, March, San Francisco.

Berlak, A., and H. Berlak. 1981. *Dilemmas of schooling: Teaching and social change.* London: Methuen.

———. 1987. Teachers working with teachers to transform schools. In *Educating teachers: Changing the nature of pedagogical knowledge,* ed. J. Smyth, 169–178. London: The Falmer Press.

Berthoff, A. E. 1981. *The making of meaning: Metaphors, models, and maxims for writing teachers.* Portsmouth, NH: Boynton/Cook Publishers.

———. 1982. *Forming, thinking, writing: The composing imagination.* Portsmouth, NH: Boynton/Cook Publishers.

———. 1987a. Dialectical notebooks and the audit of meaning. In *The journal book,* ed. T. Fulwiler, 11–18. Portsmouth, NH: Boynton/Cook Publishers.

———. 1987b. The teacher as REsearcher. In *Reclaiming the classroom: Teacher research as an agency for change,* ed. D. Goswami and P. R. Stillman, 28–38. Portsmouth, NH: Boynton/Cook Publishers.

Bissex, G. L., and R. H. Bullock, eds. 1987. *Seeing for ourselves:*

Case-study research by teachers of writing. Portsmouth, NH: Heinemann.

Blair, C. P. 1988. Only one of the voices: Dialogic writing across the curriculum. *College English* 50: 383–389.

Boomer, G. 1987. Addressing the problem of elsewhereness: A case for action research in schools. In *Reclaiming the classroom: Teacher research as an agency for change,* ed. D. Goswami and P. R. Stillman, 4–13. Portsmouth, NH: Boynton/Cook Publishers.

Bowers, C. A. 1987. *Elements of a post-liberal theory of education.* New York: Teachers College Press.

Britton, J. 1970. *Language and learning.* New York: Penguin.

––––––. 1987. A quiet form of research. In *Reclaiming the classroom: Teacher research as an agency for change,* ed. D. Goswami and P. R. Stillman, 13–19. Portsmouth, NH: Boynton/Cook Publishers.

Britzman, D. P. 1988. On educating the educators. *Harvard Educational Review* 58: 85–94.

Brodkey, L. 1987. Writing critical ethnographic narratives. *Anthropology and Education Quarterly* 18: 67–76.

––––––. 1989. On the subjects of class and gender in "The literacy letters." *College English* 51: 125–141.

Burton, F. R. 1986. A teacher's conception of the action research process. *Language Arts* 63: 718–723.

Cain, W. 1987. Education and social change. *College English* 49: 83–88.

Campbell, D. R. 1988. Collaboration and contradiction in a research and staff-development project. *Teachers College Record* 90: 99–121.

Carr, W., and S. Kemmis. 1986. *Becoming critical.* London: The Falmer Press.

Cherryholmes, C. H. 1988. *Power and criticism: Poststructural investigations in education.* New York: Teachers College Press.

Clandinin, D. J. 1986. *Classroom practice: Teacher images in action*. London: The Falmer Press.

Connelly, E. M., and D. J. Clandinin. 1988. *Teachers as curriculum planners: Narratives of experience*. New York: Teachers College Press.

Corey, S. M. 1953. *Action research to improve school practices*. New York: Teachers College Press.

deBeaugrande, R. 1988. In search of feminist discourse: The "difficult" case of Luce Irigaray. *College English* 50: 253–272.

deLauretis, T., ed. 1986. *Feminist studies, critical studies*. Bloomington: Indiana University Press.

Donmoyer, R. 1989. Theory, practice, and the double-edged problem of idiosyncracy. *Journal of Curriculum and Supervision* 4: 257–270.

Duckworth, E. 1986. Teaching as research. *Harvard Educational Review* 56: 481–495.

Dunn, S., S. Florio-Ruane, and C. M. Clark. 1985. The teacher as respondent to the high school writer. In *The acquisition of written language: Response and revision*, ed. S. W. Freedman, 33–50. Norwood, NJ: Ablex Publishing Corporation.

Elbaz, F. 1983. *Teacher thinking: A study of practical knowledge*. London: Croom Helm.

————. 1987. Teachers' knowledge of teaching: Strategies for reflection. In *Educating teachers: Changing the nature of pedagogical knowledge*, ed. J. Smyth, 45–53. London: The Falmer Press.

Elbaz, F., and R. Elbaz. 1988. Curriculum and textuality. *The Journal of Curriculum Theorizing* 8 (2): 107–131.

Elliot, J. 1989. Academics and action-research: The training workshop as an exercise in ideological deconstruction. Paper presented at Annual Meeting of American Educational Research Association, March, San Francisco.

Ellsworth, E. 1989. Why doesn't this feel empowering? Working through the repressive myths of critical pedagogy. *Harvard Educational Review* 59: 297–324.

Erickson, F. 1986. Qualitative methods in research on teaching. In *Handbook of research on teaching,* ed. M. C. Wittrock, 119–161. New York: Macmillan.

Evans, C. L., M. L. Stubbs, P. Frechette, C. Neely, and J. Warner. 1987. Educational practitioners: Absent voices in the building of educational theory. Working Paper No. 170. Wellesley, MA: Wellesley College Center for Research on Women.

Fay, B. 1975. *Social theory and political practice.* London: George Allen & Unwin.

Fine, M. 1988. Sexuality, schooling, and adolescent females: The missing discourse of desire. *Harvard Educational Review* 58: 29–53.

Firestone, W. A. 1987. Meaning in method: The rhetoric of quantitative and qualitative research. *Educational Researcher* 16(7): 16–21.

Fishman, A. R., and E. J. Raver. 1989. "Maybe I'm just NOT teacher material": Dialogue journals in the student teaching experience. *English Education* 21: 92–109.

Flinders, D. J. 1988. Teacher isolation and the new reform. *Journal of Curriculum and Supervision* 4: 17–29.

Florio-Ruane, S., and J. B. Dohanich. 1984. Research currents: Communicating findings by teacher-researcher deliberation. *Language Arts* 61: 724–730.

Freedman, S., J. Jackson, and C. Boles. 1982. *The effects of the institutional structure of schools on teachers.* Boston: Boston Women's Teachers Group.

Freedman, S. W., ed. 1985. *The acquisition of written language: Response and revision.* Norwood, NJ: Ablex Publishing Corporation.

Freire, P. 1974. *Pedagogy of the oppressed.* New York: Seabury Press.

———. 1985. *The politics of education.* South Hadley, MA: Bergin and Garvey Publishers, Inc.

Fullan, M. 1982. *The meaning of educational change.* New York: Teachers College Press.

Fulwiler, T. 1982. Writing: An act of cognition. In *Teaching writing in all disciplines,* ed. C. W. Griffin, 15–26. San Francisco: Jossey-Bass Inc., Publishers.

———. 1987a. *Teaching with writing.* Portsmouth, NH: Boynton/ Cook Publishers.

———, ed. 1987b. *The journal book.* Portsmouth, NH: Boynton/Cook Publishers.

Giroux, H. A. 1988. Liberal arts, teaching, and critical literacy: Toward a definition of school as a form of cultural politics. In *Contemporary curriculum discourses,* ed. W. F. Pinar, 243–263. Scottsdale, AZ: Gorsuch Scarisbrick, Publishers.

Gitlin, A., M. Siegel, and K. Boru. 1988. Purpose and method: Rethinking the use of ethnography by the educational left. Paper presented at Annual Meeting of American Educational Research Association, April, New Orleans.

Glatthorn, A. A. 1987. Cooperative professional development: Peer-centered options for teacher growth. *Educational Leadership* 45 (3): 31–35.

Goodman, J. 1988. The disenfranchisement of elementary teachers and strategies for resistance. *Journal of Curriculum and Supervision* 3: 201–220.

Goswami, D., and P. R. Stillman, eds. 1987. *Reclaiming the classroom: Teacher research as an agency for change.* Portsmouth, NH: Boynton/Cook Publishers.

Graybeal, J. 1987. The team journal. In *The journal book,* ed. T. Fulwiler, 306–311. Portsmouth, NH: Boynton/Cook Publishers.

Greene, M. 1986a. In search of a critical pedagogy. *Harvard Educational Review* 56: 427–441.

184

_____. 1986b. Reflection and passion in teaching. *Journal of Curriculum and Supervision* 2: 68–81.

_____. 1988. *The dialectic of freedom.* New York: Teachers College Press.

_____. 1990. Interpretation and re-vision: Toward another story. In *Teaching and thinking about curriculum: Critical inquiries,* ed. J. Sears and J. D. Marshall, 75–78. New York: Teachers College Press.

Gregory, R. P. 1988. *Action research in the secondary school.* New York: Routledge.

Grumet, M. R. 1987. The politics of personal knowledge. *Curriculum Inquiry* 17: 319–329.

_____. 1988a. *Bitter milk: Women and teaching.* Amherst: University of Massachusetts Press.

_____. 1988b. On daffodils that come before the swallow dares. Paper presented to Conference on Qualitative Inquiry, June, Stanford University.

_____. 1989. Dinner at Abigail's: Nurturing collaboration. *NEA Today: Issues '89* 7 (6): 20–25.

Harding, S. 1986. *The science question in feminism.* Ithaca, NY: Cornell University Press.

_____, ed. 1987. *Feminism and methodology.* Bloomington: Indiana University Press.

Harris, J. 1989. The idea of community in the study of writing. *College Composition and Communication* 40: 11–22.

Heath, S. B. 1983. *Ways with words: Language, life, and work in communities and classrooms.* Cambridge: Cambridge University Press.

_____. 1987. A lot of talk about nothing. In *Reclaiming the classroom: Teacher research as an agency for change,* ed. D. Goswami and P. R. Stillman, 39–48. Portsmouth, NH: Boynton/Cook Publishers.

Heath, S. B., and A. Branscombe. 1985. "Intelligent writing" in an audience community: Teacher, students, and researcher. In *The acquisition of written language,* ed. S. W. Freedman, 3–32. Norwood, NJ: Ablex Publishing Corporation.

Hitchcock, G., and D. Hughes. 1989. *Research and the teacher: A qualitative introduction to school-based research.* New York: Routledge.

Hoffman, N. 1981. *Women's "true" profession: Voices from the history of teaching.* New York: The Feminist Press.

Holly, M. L. 1989. *Writing to grow: Keeping a personal-professional journal.* Portsmouth, NH: Heinemann.

Hopkins, D. 1985. *A teacher's guide to classroom research.* Philadelphia: Open University Press.

_____. 1987. Teacher research as a basis for staff development. In *Staff development for school improvement: A focus on the teacher,* ed. M. F. Wideen and I. Andrews, 111–128. London: The Falmer Press.

Huebner, D. 1987. The vocation of teaching. In *Teacher renewal: Professional issues, personal choices,* ed. F. Bolin and J. M. Falk, 17–29. New York: Teachers College Press.

Jacob, E. 1987. Qualitative research traditions: A review. *Review of Educational Research* 57: 1–50.

Jenkinson, E. B. 1988. Learning to write, writing to learn. *Phi Delta Kappan* 69: 712–717.

Kemmis, S., and R. McTaggart. 1982. *The action research planner.* Geelong, Australia: Deakin University Press.

Kirby, D., D. Latta, and R. Vinz. 1988. Beyond interior decorating: Using writing to make meaning in the elementary school. *Phi Delta Kappan* 69: 718–724.

Knoblauch, C. H. 1988. Rhetorical constructions: Dialogue and commitment. *College English* 50: 125–140.

Kohli, W. 1989. Education and freedom in the American experience:

Critical imagination as pedagogy. *Harvard Educational Review* 59: 98–107.

Krall, F. R. 1988. From the inside out: Personal history as educational research. *Educational Theory* 38: 467–479.

Laird, S. 1988. Reforming "women's true profession": A case for "feminist pedagogy" in teacher education? *Harvard Educational Review* 58: 449–463.

Lampert, M. 1985. How do teachers manage to teach? Perspectives on problems in practice. *Harvard Educational Review* 55: 178–194.

Lather, P. 1986. Research as *praxis*. *Harvard Educational Review* 56: 257–277.

———. 1988. Educational research and practice in a postmodern era. Paper presented at Annual Meeting of American Educational Research Association, April, New Orleans.

———. 1989a. Deconstructing/deconstructive inquiry: The politics of knowing and being known. Paper presented at Annual Meeting of American Educational Research Association, March, San Francisco.

———. 1989b. Reinscribing otherwise: The play of values in the practices of the human sciences. Paper presented at Invitational Conference on Alternative Paradigms for Inquiry, March, San Francisco.

LeFevre, K. 1987. *Invention as a social act.* Carbondale: Southern Illinois University Press.

Lewis, M., and R. I. Simon. 1986. A discourse not intended for her: Learning and teaching within patriarchy. *Harvard Educational Review* 56: 457–472.

Lieberman, A. 1986. Collaborative work. *Educational Leadership* 43 (5): 4–8.

Lumley, D. 1987. An analysis of peer group dialogue journals for classroom use. In *Reclaiming the classroom: Teacher research as an agency for change,* ed. D. Goswami and P. R. Stillman, 169–177. Portsmouth, NH: Boynton/Cook Publishers.

Maeroff, G. I. 1988. A blueprint for empowering teachers. *Phi Delta Kappan* 69: 473–477.

Maher, F., and M. K. Tetreault. 1988. Breaking through illusion II: The intersection of feminist pedagogy and feminist ethnography. Paper presented at Annual Meeting of American Educational Research Association, April, New Orleans.

Marcus, G. E., and M. Fischer. 1986. *Anthropology as cultural critique: An experimental moment in the human sciences.* Chicago: University of Chicago Press.

Martens, M. L. 1988. Implementation of a problem-solving curriculum in elementary science: Case studies of teachers in change. Doctoral diss., St. John's University, New York.

Martin, B., and C. Mohanty. 1986. Feminist politics: What's home got to do with it? In *Feminist studies, critical studies,* ed. T. deLauretis, 191–212. Bloomington: Indiana University Press.

May, N. 1982. The teacher-as-researcher movement in Britain. In *Conceptions of curriculum knowledge: Focus on students and teachers,* ed. W. Schubert and A. Schubert, 23–30. State College: Pennsylvania State University Press.

McKernan, J. 1988. The countenance of curriculum action research: Traditional, collaborative, and emancipatory-critical conceptions. *Journal of Curriculum and Supervision* 3: 173–200.

McLaren, P. 1989. *Life in schools: An introduction to critical pedagogy in the foundations of education.* New York: Longman.

McNeil, L. M. 1986. *Contradictions of control: School structure and school knowledge.* London: Routledge and Kegan Paul.

Messer-Davidow, E. 1985. Knowers, knowing, knowledge: Feminist theory and education. *Journal of Thought* 20: 8–24.

Miller, J. L. 1986. Women as teachers: Enlarging conversations on issues of gender and self-concept. *Journal of Curriculum and Supervision* 1: 111–121.

_____. 1987. Teachers' emerging texts: The empowering potential of writing inservice. In *Educating teachers: Changing the nature of pedagogical knowledge,* ed. J. Smyth, 193–206. London: The Falmer Press.

_____. 1988. The resistance of women academics: An autobiographical account. In *Contemporary curriculum discourses,* ed. W. F. Pinar, 486–494. Scottsdale, AZ: Gorsuch Scarisbrick, Publishers.

_____. 1990. Teachers as curriculum creators. In *Teaching and thinking about curriculum: Critical inquiries,* ed. J. Sears and J. D. Marshall, 85–96. New York: Teachers College Press.

Mischler, E. G. 1979. Meaning in context: Is there any other kind? *Harvard Educational Review* 49: 1–18.

Moffett, J. 1968. *Teaching the universe of discourse.* Boston: Houghton-Mifflin.

_____. 1981. *Active voice: A writing program across the curriculum.* Portsmouth, NH: Boynton/Cook Publishers.

_____. 1985. Hidden impediments to improving English teaching. *Phi Delta Kappan* 67: 52–55.

_____. 1988. *Coming on center: Essays in English education.* Portsmouth, NH: Boynton/Cook Publishers.

Mohr, M., and M. MacLean. 1987. *Working together: A guide for teacher-researchers.* Urbana, IL: National Council of Teachers of English.

Mooney, R. 1975. The researcher himself. In *Curriculum theorizing: The reconceptualists,* ed. W. F. Pinar, 175–207. Berkeley, CA: McCutchan Publishing Corporation.

Morton, D., and M. Zavarzadeh. 1989. The cultural politics of the fiction workshop. *Cultural Critique* 11: 155–173.

Myers, M. 1985. *The teacher-researcher: How to study writing in the classroom.* Urbana, IL: National Council of Teachers of English.

Newman, J. M. 1988. Sharing journals: Conversational mirrors for seeing ourselves as learners, writers, and teachers. *English Education* 20: 134–156.

Newton, J., and N. Hoffman, eds. 1988. Preface. *Feminist Studies* 14: 3–9.

Nias, J., and S. Groundwater-Smith. 1988. *The enquiring teacher: Supporting and sustaining teacher research.* London: The Falmer Press.

Oakes, J., S. E. Hare, and K. A. Sirotnik. 1986. Collaborative inquiry: A congenial paradigm in a cantankerous world. *Teachers College Record* 87: 545–561.

Pagano, J. 1988a. The claim of philia. In *Contemporary curriculum discourses,* ed. W. F. Pinar, 514–530. Scottsdale, AZ: Gorsuch Scarisbrick, Publishers.

———. 1988b. Teaching women. *Educational Theory* 38: 321–339.

———. 1990. *Exiles and community: Teaching in the patriarchal wilderness.* Albany: State University of New York Press.

Patai, D. 1988. Constructing a self: A Brazilian life story. *Feminist Studies* 14: 143–166.

Perl, S., and N. Wilson. 1986. *Through teachers' eyes: Portraits of writing teachers at work.* Portsmouth, NH: Heinemann Educational Books, Inc.

Peyton, J. K., and M. Seyoum. 1989. The effect of teacher strategies on students' interactive writing: The case of dialogue journals. *Research in the Teaching of English* 23: 310–334.

Pinar, W. F., ed. 1975. *Curriculum theorizing: The reconceptualists.* Berkeley, CA: McCutchan Publishing Corporation.

———, ed., 1988. *Contemporary curriculum discourses.* Scottsdale, AZ: Gorsuch Scarisbrick, Publishers.

Pinar, W. F., and M. R. Grumet. 1976. *Toward a poor curriculum.* Dubuque, IA: Kendall/Hunt.

———. 1988. Socratic *Caesura* and the theory-practice relationship. In *Contemporary curriculum discourses,* ed. W. F. Pinar, 92–100. Scottsdale, AZ: Gorsuch Scarisbrick, Publishers.

Porter, A. C. 1987. Teacher collaboration: New partnerships to attack old problems. *Phi Delta Kappan* 69: 147–152.

Powdermaker, H. 1966. *Stranger and friend: The way of the anthropologist.* New York: W. W. Norton.

Progoff, I. 1975. *At a journal workshop.* New York: Dialogue House.

Radford-Hill, S. 1986. Considering feminism as a model for social change. In *Feminist studies, critical studies,* ed. T. de Lauretis, 157–172. Bloomington: Indiana University Press.

Ranells, E. 1989. The dynamics of the interactive inservice process in the personalization of the curriculum: Case studies of special education teachers. Doctoral diss., St. John's University, New York.

Richardson, L. 1988. The collective story: Postmodernism and the writing of sociology. *Sociological Focus* 21: 199–208.

Roderick, J. A. 1986. Dialogue writing: Context for reflecting on self as teacher and researcher. *Journal of Curriculum and Supervision* 1: 305–315.

Roderick, J. A., and L. M. Berman. 1984. Dialoguing about dialogue journals. *Language Arts* 61: 686–692.

Roman, L. G., and M. W. Apple. 1988. Is naturalism a move away from positivism? Materialist and feminist approaches to subjectivity in ethnographic research. Paper presented to the Qualitative Inquiry Conference, June, Stanford University.

Roman, L. G., and L. K. Christian-Smith, eds. 1988. *Becoming feminine: The politics of popular culture.* London: The Falmer Press.

Rudduck, J. 1988. Changing the world of the classroom by understanding it: A review of some aspects of the work of Lawrence Stenhouse. *Journal of Curriculum and Supervision* 4: 30–42.

Rudduck, J., and D. Hopkins, eds. 1985. *Research as a basis for teaching: Readings from the work of Lawrence Stenhouse.* Portsmouth, NH: Boynton/Cook Publishers.

Schön, D. A. 1983. *The reflective practitioner: How professionals think in action.* New York: Basic Books, Inc.

————. 1987. *Educating the reflective practitioner: Toward a new design for teaching and learning in the professions.* San Francisco: Jossey-Bass Publishers.

Schubert, W. H. 1986. *Curriculum: Perspective, paradigm, and possibility.* New York: Macmillan.

Sears, J. T., and J. D. Marshall, eds. 1990. *Teaching and thinking about curriculum: Critical inquiries.* New York: Teachers College Press.

Seifert, G. 1988. A multiple case study of the effects of reflective writing of elementary school children in individual counseling with a school psychologist. Doctoral diss., St. John's University, New York.

Shuy, R. W. 1987. Research currents: Dialogue as the heart of learning. *Language Arts* 64: 890–897.

Simon, R. I. 1987. Empowerment as a pedagogy of possibility. *Language Arts* 64: 370–382.

Smith, J. K., and L. Heshusius. 1986. Closing down the conversation: The end of the quantitative-qualitative debate among educational inquirers. *Educational Researcher* 15: 4–13.

Smith, M. L. 1987. Publishing qualitative research. *American Educational Research Journal* 24: 173–184.

Smith, S. C. 1987. The collaborative school takes shape. *Educational Leadership* 45 (3): 4–6.

Smyth, J. 1987a. *A rationale for teachers' critical pedagogy: A Handbook.* Geelong, Australia: Deakin University Press.

————, ed. 1987b. *Educating teachers: Changing the nature of pedagogical knowledge.* London: The Falmer Press.

Staton, J. 1980. Writing and counseling: Using a dialogue journal. *Language Arts* 57: 514–518.

————. 1987. The power of responding in dialogue journals. In *The journal book,* ed. T. Fulwiler, 47–63. Portsmouth, NH: Boynton/ Cook Publishers.

Staton, J., R. Shuy, J. K. Payton, and L. Reed. 1988. *Dialogue journal communication: Classroom, linguistic, social, and cognitive views.* Norwood, NJ: Ablex Publishing Corp.

Stenhouse, L. 1985. Research as a basis for teaching. In *Research as a basis for teaching,* ed. J. Rudduck and D. Hopkins, 113–128. Portsmouth, NH: Boynton/Cook Publishers.

———. 1988. Artistry and teaching: The teacher as focus of research and development. *Journal of Curriculum and Supervision* 4: 43–51.

Sullivan, E. V., S. Martinic, and H. Walker. 1987. Critical interpretation: A comparison of two ethnographies. *Phenomenology + Pedagogy* 5: 242–267.

Tabakin, G., and K. Densmore. 1986. Teacher professionalization and gender analysis. *Teachers College Record* 88: 257–279.

Tom, A. R. 1985. Inquiring into inquiry-oriented teacher education. *Journal of Teacher Education* (September-October): 35–44.

Tripp, D. H. 1987. Teachers, journals and collaborative research. In *Educating teachers: Changing the nature of pedagogical knowledge,* ed. J. Smyth, 179–192. London: The Falmer Press.

Van Maanen, J. 1988. *Tales of the field: On writing ethnography.* Chicago: The University of Chicago Press.

van Manen, M. 1988. The relation between research and pedagogy. In *Contemporary curriculum discourses,* ed. W. F. Pinar, 437–452. Scottsdale, AZ: Gorsuch Scarisbrick, Publishers.

Weedon, C. 1987. *Feminist practice and poststructuralist theory.* New York: Basil Blackwell.

Weiler, K. 1988. *Women teaching for change.* South Hadley, MA: Bergin and Garvey Publishers, Inc.

Welch, S. 1985. *Communities of resistance and solidarity: A feminist theology of liberation.* New York: Orbis.

Wigginton, E. 1989. Foxfire grows up. *Harvard Educational Review* 59: 24–49.

Wood, G. 1990. Teachers as curriculum workers. In *Teaching and thinking about curriculum: Critical inquiries,* ed. J. Sears and J. D. Marshall, 97–109. New York: Teachers College Press.

Zagarell, S. A. 1988. Narrative of community: The identification of a genre. *Signs: Journal of Women in Culture and Society* 13: 498–527.

Zeichner, K. M., and D. P. Liston. 1987. Teaching student teachers to reflect. *Harvard Educational Review* 57: 23–48.

INDEX